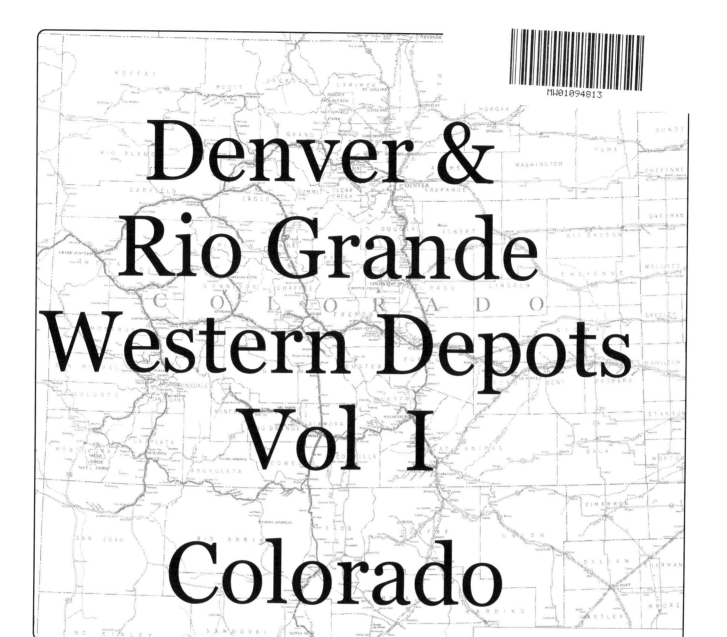

Denver & Rio Grande Western Depots Vol I Colorado

CLIVE CARTER
&
DAVID CARTER

ISBN: 1490936203
ISBN-13: 13:978-1490936208

Contents

INTRODUCTION

This book is the first of two volumes that describe the depots owned by the Denver and Rio Grande Western Railroad. Volume I covers the majority of the buildings in the state of Colorado. The remainder of the D&RGW Colorado depots and those in Utah, together with depots operated by the Rio Grande Southern and Denver & Salt Lake Railroads, are addressed in Volume II. Depots in Colorado belonging to other railroads (UP, AT&SF, CBQ, C&S and smaller railroads) are summarized in Volume III.

Descriptions of the structures, complemented by drawings of them, are presented. Basic information includes the dates of their construction and retirement. Information was collected from several sources, The predominant source was the Interstate Commerce Commission Survey Reports prepared on site by the Commission's Field Engineers in c1920 as part of the Valuation process. The engineers generated a detail description of each structure, usually including a hand drawn plan and cross section(s). The drawings are reproduced herein. The position of windows or doors in their drawings was not illustrated because such information was not pertinent to the Valuation process.

We have also made reference to Valuation update reports prepared by the railroad periodically between 1920 and 1980 for the ICC. Basically, an update was a compilation of the railroad's Authorities For Expenditure for work completed during the reporting period. Information with respect to structural modifications made to individual structures and their eventual disposal was collected in this way. Drawings of buildings constructed after 1920, when found in company records, were also used.

Other sources consulted included the construction and changes book started in 1890 by the Denver and Rio Grande Railroad Bridges & Buildings Department, and a D&RG 1892 list of structures and their overall dimensions. Sanborn Fire Insurance maps helped to clarify construction dates for several depots built in the 1880's.

Plat maps presented herein depict the location of each depot in relation to the main track; not all secondary tracks are necessarily shown. Nearby water tanks, stockyards and engine houses are noted.

The single word "Depot" is used throughout the book to identify a combination passenger and freight structure having facilities for both types of service. The terms "Passenger Depot" and "Freight Depot" are used to identify to identify a building having a specific function. Where a new depot replaced another, data for both is presented in chronological order. Similarly. passenger buildings are listed before freight for each location. At certain points a simple shelter shed, often a converted freight car body, sufficed for passengers and freight. They are omitted here.

OVERLAND PARK TO SALIDA

Miles from Denver
to:

Overland Park....... 6.05	Eden.................... 110.56
Military Park......... 8.95	Eighth St. Pueblo.. 116.70
Fort Logan............. 9.95	Pueblo Union........ 118.38
Littleton................ 10.28	Swallows............... 134.60
Acequia................. 17.29	Beaver.................. 142.69
Louviers............... 20.74	Concrete............... 144.43
Sedaila.................. 24.53	Florence................ 151.91
Castle Rock........... 32.05	Canon City............. 160.03
Larkspur............... 42.32	Gorge.................... 164.76
Palmer Lake.......... 51.32	Parkdale................ 171.17
Monument............ 55.03	Echo..................... 179.95
Colorado Springs... 74.03	Texas Creek........... 174.11
Husted................... ?	Cotopaxi............... 191.68
Kelker................... 78.73	Howard................. 203.40
Fountain............... 86.86	Welsville............... 208.89
Buttes................... 92.41	Otis...................... 210.62
Wigwam................ 98.01	Salida................... 215.11
Piñon.................... 104.28	

PASSENGER DEPOT

Built: 1880.
Construction: Two-story lava-stone building, 350' and 260' on the west and east ends, respectively. Consisting of a central (waiting room) portion surmounted by a tower with wings 60' wide.

FREIGHT DEPOT

Built: 1902.
Construction: Office 48' x 82' with tile roof attached to a 48' x 400' freight room.
Roof: Composition.
Walls: Brick.

FRAME WAREHOUSE

48' x 160' was attached to the freight room. Granite was used for a height of 5'.
The Freight depot was at 13th and Wazee St and was retired in 1978.

Denver Union Station, CO

The central portion was rebuilt during 1914-16. The new central portion was 140'X165' and three stories high.

Doing so the wings were left undisturbed except for revision of interior arrangement and construction of a 95' extension to the east wing.

Brick walls were faced with brown sandstone for 5' above the foundation with gray terracotta above, except on the front.

Overland Park, CO

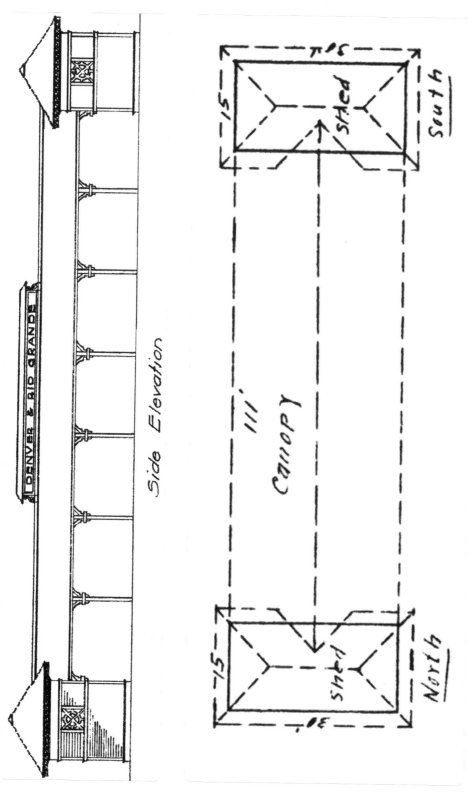

Side Elevation

DENVER & RIO GRANDE

Shed — South

15 — 30'

Canopy — 111'

Shed — North

15 — 30'

DEPOT

To Denver

FIRST PASSENGER DEPOT

Built: 1890.
Construction: Frame pavilion 16' x 172', with platform and bridge 16' x 123'
Roof: Corrugated iron.

Destroyed by fire November 12 1905.

SECOND PASSENGER DEPOT

Built: 1908.
Frame 15' x 30' depot with 15' x 111' pavilion connecting to an express room of 15' x 30'.
Roof: Hip, wood shingles.
Walls: Drop siding on both sheds.

Retired: 1930.

Military Park, CO

ELEVATION Not Available

<u>DEPOT</u>

Built: 1890.
Construction: Frame pavilion 16' x 21', with two additions of 8' x 18'.

Destroyed by fire.

Fort Logan, CO

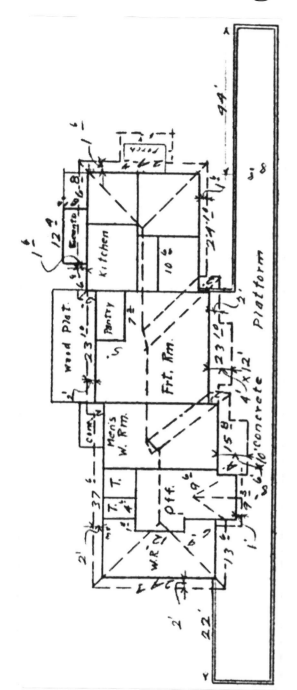

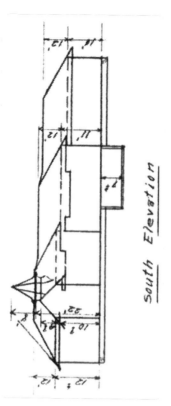

South Elevation

JOHN ST.

SHERIDAN

HOWARD AVE.

DEPOT

To Denver →

DEPOT

Built: 1889.
Construction: One-story frame of 24' x 38', with 14' x 14', 14' x 9' and 24' x 25' additions.
Roof: Hip, wood shingles.
Walls: Lap siding with 3' beaded wainscot.

Retired 1937.

Littleton, Co

PASSENGER DEPOT

Built: Before 1880.
Construction: One-story stone 24' x 40' building.
Toilets added 1915.
Roof: Gable, corrugated iron.
Walls: Stone.

Stone depot remains at Littleton RTD station.

FREIGHT DEPOT

Built: 1907.
Construction: One-story frame structure of 22' x 36'.
Roof: Hip, corrugated iron.
Walls: Cement with plaster finish.

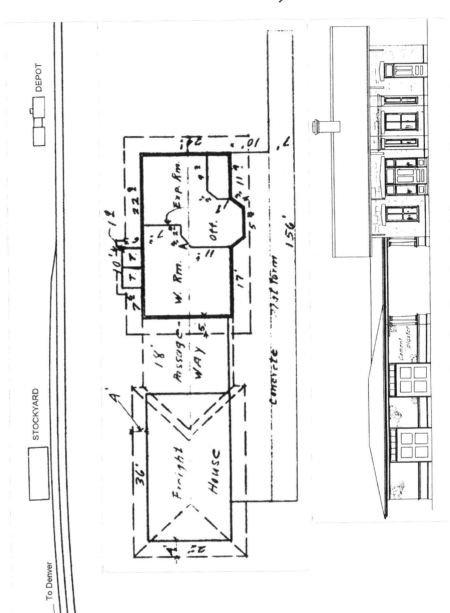

10

Acequia, CO

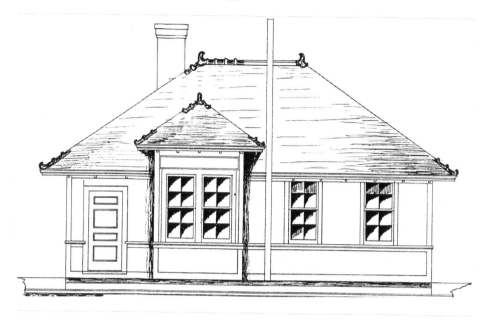

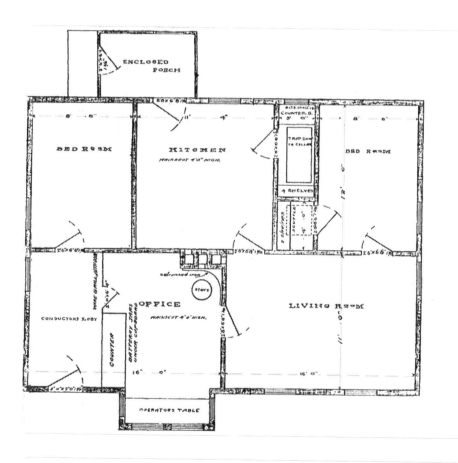

To Denver ⟶

▢ Depot

ELEVATION: 5533'

FIRST DEPOT

Built: 1903.
Construction: One-story frame of 30' x 34', with a 20' x 30' addition.

Moved to Louviers 1907.

SECOND DEPOT
Built: 1919.
Construction: One-story frame structure of 24' x 33'.
Roof: Hip, wood shingles.
Walls: Lap siding.

Retired 1937.

Louviers, CO

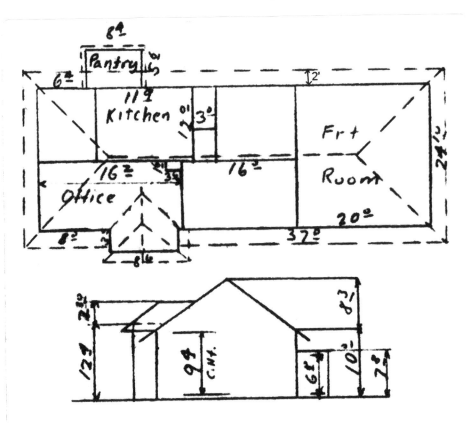

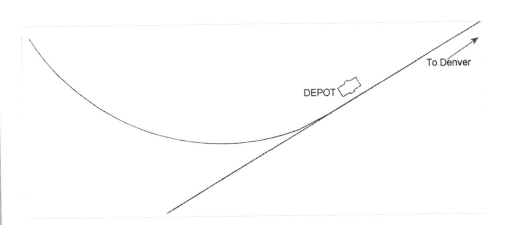

Sedalia, CO

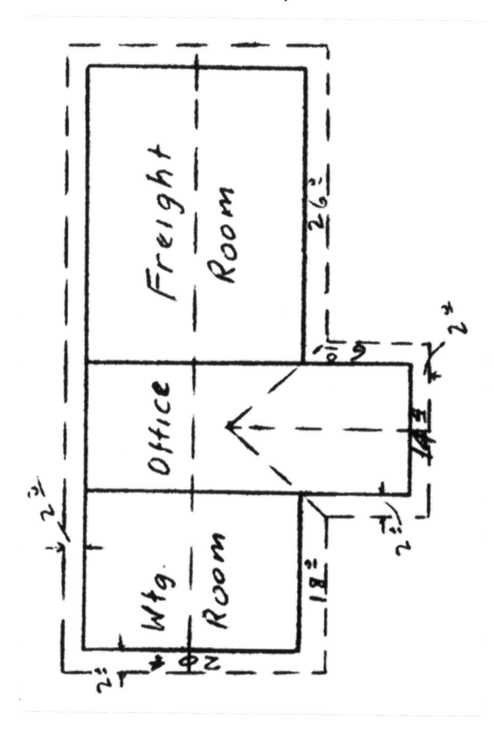

Freight Room

Office

Wtg. Room

26'

5'

9'0"

14'

2'1½"

2'3½"

18½"

2'0"

2'1"

DEPOT

To Denver ——→

STOCKYARD

PASSENGER DEPOT

Built: 1905.
Construction: One-story frame of 20' x 58' with a 14' x 30' pavilion.
Roof: Gable, wood shingles.
Walls: Lap siding.

Pavilion removed by 1920.
Frame roof added over platform in 1936.

Retired in 1955

DEPOT

Built: Prior to 1880.
Construction: One-story stone structure of 24' x 40'. 3' x 12' bay window added in 1906.
Roof: Gable, corrugated iron.
Walls: Stone.

Retired 1970.

Castle Rock, CO

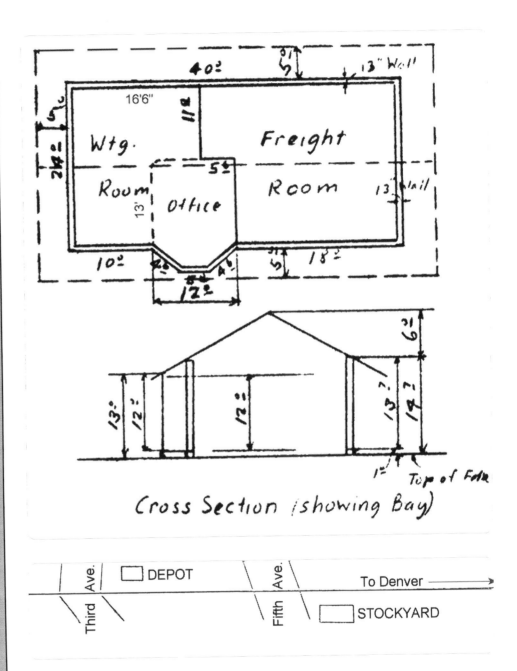

Cross Section (showing Bay)

Larkspur, CO

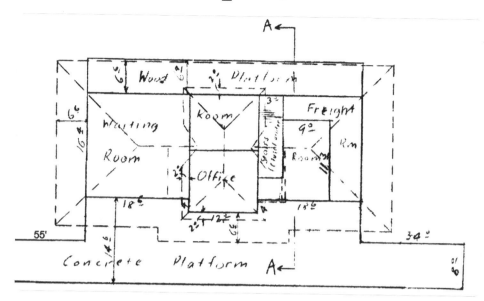

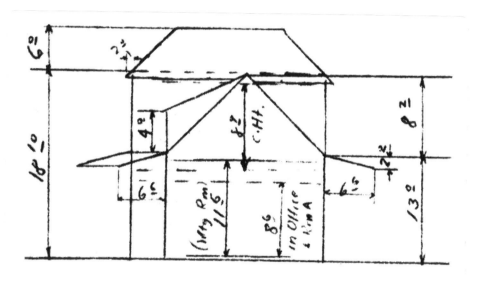

Section A-A

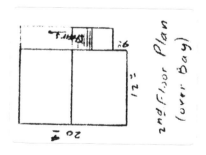

2nd Floor Plan (over Bay)

TANK   DEPOT   STOCKYARD   To Denver

ELEVATION 6668'

DEPOT

Built: 1883.
One and one-half story, frame 16' x 49' structure, with 4' x 12' addition.
Roof: Hip, wood shingles.
Walls: Shiplap with 3' beaded wainscot.

Partially retired in 1951.
Remainder converted to section house.

Palmer Lake, CO

ELEVATION ~5,325'.

PASSENGER DEPOT

Built: 1882.
Construction: One
story frame 22' x 22'.
Additions of 16' x 18'
prior to 1891 then 16' x
20' in 1903.
Roof: Hip, gable and
tower, wood shingles.
Walls: Shiplap; a 4"
belt molding formed
window sills.

Retired 1940.

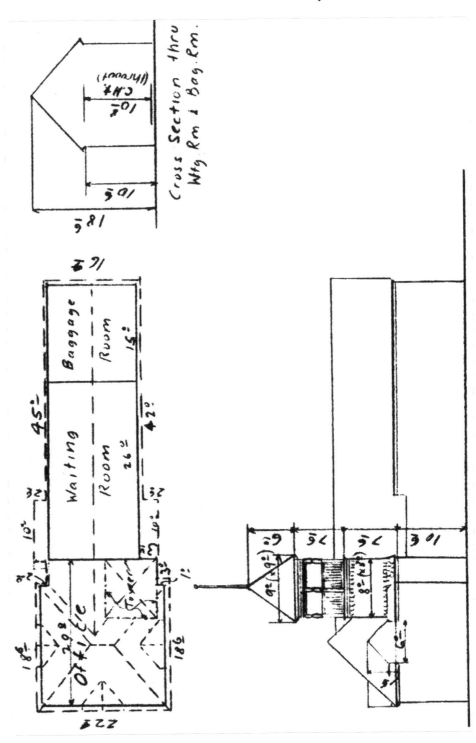

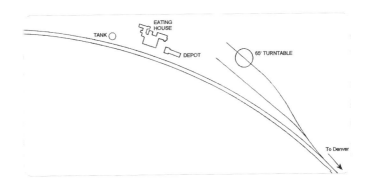

16

Monument, CO

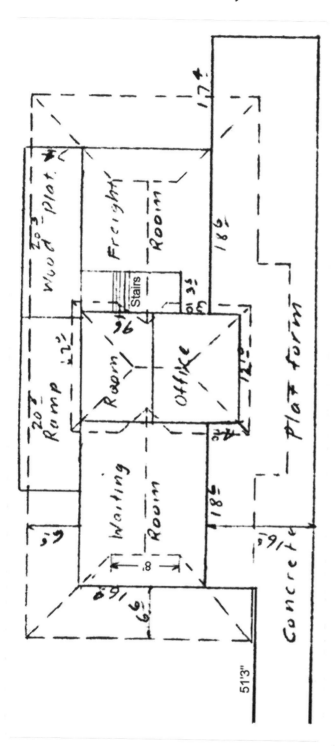

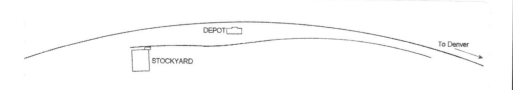

DEPOT

Built: 1883.
One and one-half story frame 13' x 16.
Additions: two 16' x 19' extensions and a 4' x 13' bay window.
Similar to Larkspur depot.
Roof: Hip, metal.
Walls: Shiplap with 3' beaded wainscot.

Retired 1948.

ELEVATION 6100'

PASSENGER DEPOT

Built: 1887.
Construction: One-story stone structure of 31' x 59'6" Additions of 8'6" x 27' and 12'X20' (porch) and pavilions at east and west end.

Enlarged with bay window 1911.
Enlarged and altered 1919.

BAGGAGE & EXPRESS ADDITION

Built: 1901.
Construction: Baggage room of 40' x 80' and express building of 30' x 102'. Office of 40'5" x 15' added in 1926.

Retired 1972.

FREIGHT DEPOT 1

Built: 1886.
Construction: Frame structure of 32' x 100.

Retired 1901.

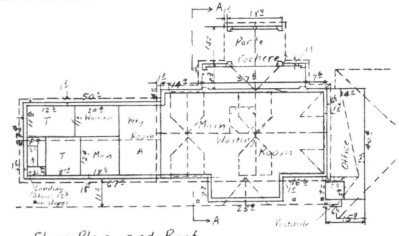

Floor Plan and Roof of Main Bldg.

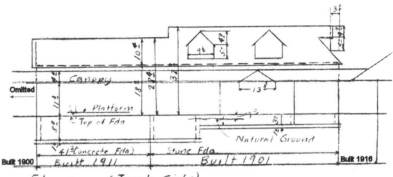

Elevation (Track Side)

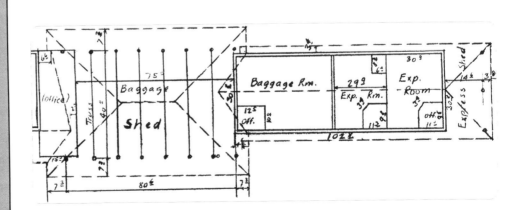

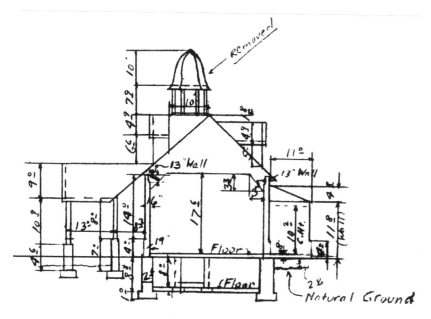

SECTION 'A-A'

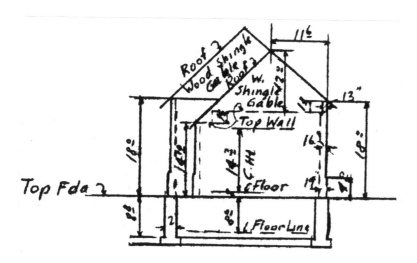

Elevation North End
of Depot

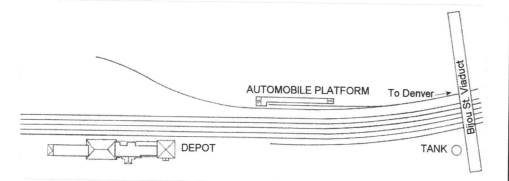

FREIGHT DEPOT 2

Built: 1901.
Construction: Brick
structure of 32' x 142'.

Retired 1962.

ELEVATION 6596'

DEPOT

Built: 1883.
Construction: One-
story frame structure
of 16' x 68'.
(No depot plan
available.)

Destroyed by fire 1907.
Replaced 1907 by two
car bodies.

Retired 1956.

Husted, CO

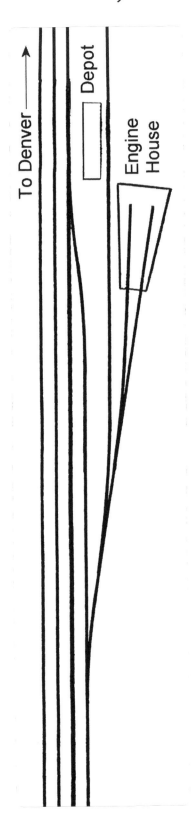

Kelker, CO

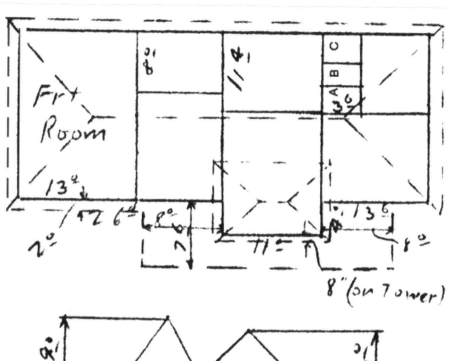

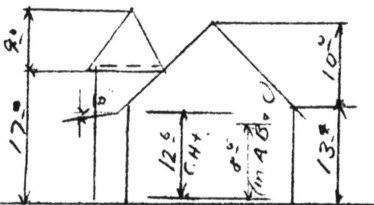

 Depot

To Denver ⟶

ELEVATION 5849'

DEPOT

Built: 1888.
Construction: One-story frame structure of 24' x 50', with a 4' x 11' addition.
Roof: Hip, wood shingles.
Tower: Wood shingles.
Walls: Lap siding with 3'2" M&B wainscot.

Retired 1955.

ELEVATION 5577'

PASSENGER DEPOT

Built: 1890.
Construction: One-story frame of 24' x 81', with a 4' x 11' addition.
Roof: Gable, wood shingles.
Tower: Wood shingles.
Walls: Lap siding.

Retired 1962.

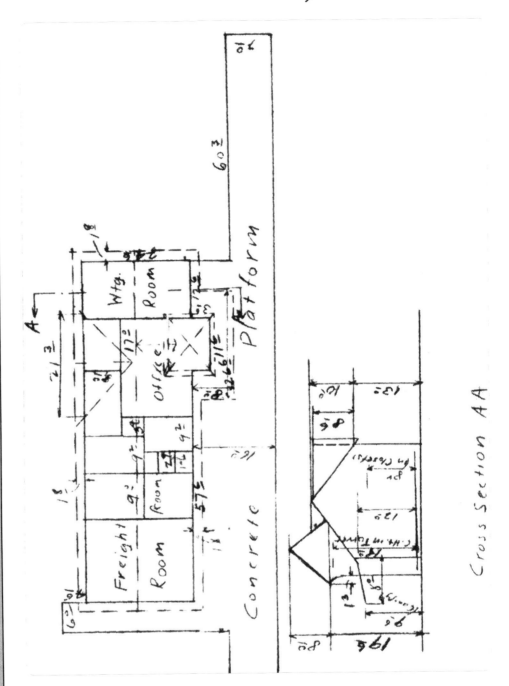

Buttes, CO

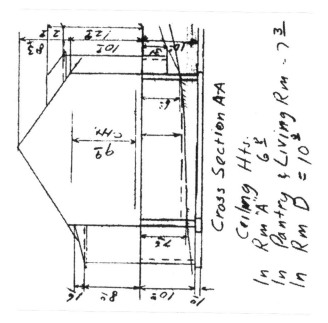

Cross Section AA

Ceiling Hts.
In Rm "A" 6'²
In Pantry & Living Rm - 7' 3
In Rm D = 10' 3

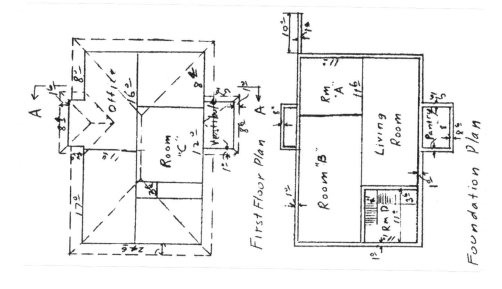

First Floor Plan

Foundation Plan

Depot

To Denver →

FIRST DEPOT

Reported in 1891.
Construction:
Structure of 16' x 44'.

SECOND DEPOT

Built: By early 1900's.
Construction: Two-story frame structure of 24' x 33'.
Roof: Hip, wood shingles.
Walls: Wood shingles with 3'6" lap siding wainscot.

Moved to Pinon 1939.

Wigwam, CO

DEPOT

Built: 1902.
Construction: One-story frame structure of 24' x 34'.
Roof: Hip, wood shingles.
Walls: Wood shingles with 3'6" lap siding wainscot.

Retired 1948.

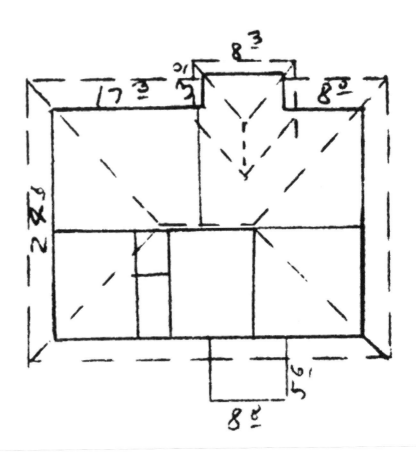

←—To Denver

DEPOT

24

Pinon, CO

To Denver →

DEPOT

TANK

FIRST DEPOT

Built: 1890.
Construction: One-story frame of 12' x 35', with 12' x 16' and 6' x 9' additions.

Destroyed by fire 10 July 1915.
Replaced by two car bodies.

SECOND DEPOT

Built: Unknown.
Moved from Buttes 1939.
Construction: Two-story frame of 24' x 33'.

Eden, CO

FIRST DEPOT

Built: 1888.
Construction: One-story 24' x 51' depot with 4' x 11' addition.

SECOND DEPOT

Built: 1901.
Construction: One-story frame structure of 24' x 36'; possibly first depot rebuilt.
Roof: Gable, composite shingles.
Walls: Board and batten.

Converted to section house by 1923.

SECTION HOUSE
(EX-DEPOT)

To Denver →

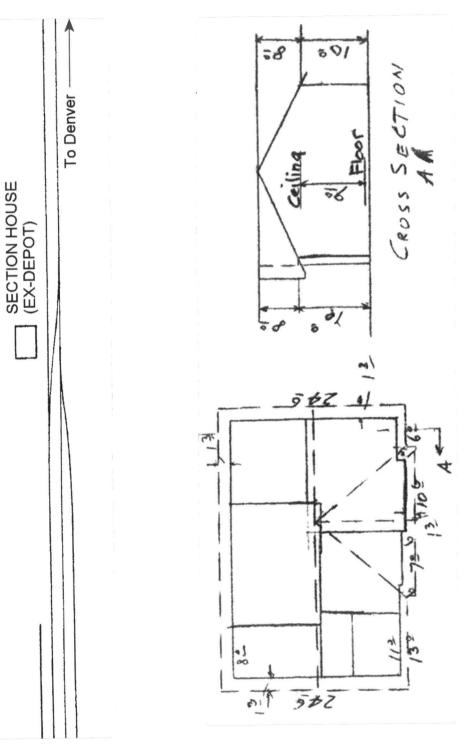

Eighth St. Pueblo, CO

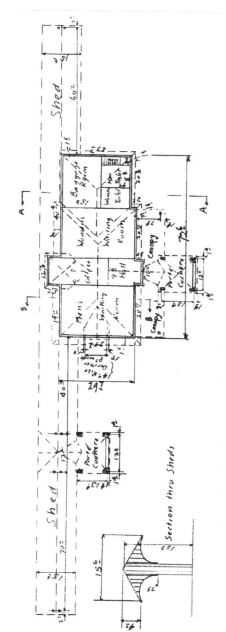

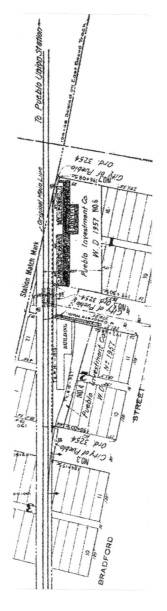

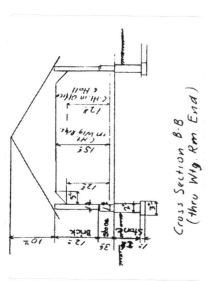

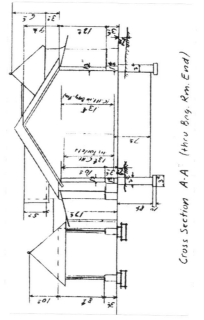

ELEVATION 4688'

PASSENGER DEPOT

Built: 1889.
Construction: One-story depot 29' x 72'. With wood sheds.
Roof: Hip, wood shingles.
Walls: Brick.

Retired 1936.

FREIGHT DEPOT

Built: 1890.
Construction: One-story structure of 40' x 292', and brick two-story structure of 42'X40' in freight yard. Subsequent freight house jointly owned and operated with Missouri Pacific RR.

Retired 1926.

Pueblo Union, CO

DEPOT & HOTEL

Built: Not Available.
Construction: Frame structure of 26' x 54'. With 6' x 12', 31' x 66', 14' x 16' and 11' x 26' additions.

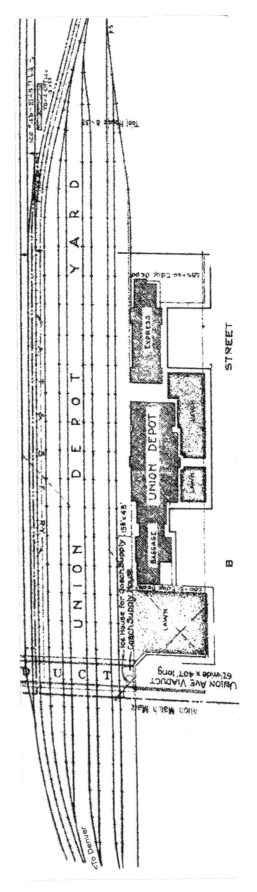

Swallows, CO

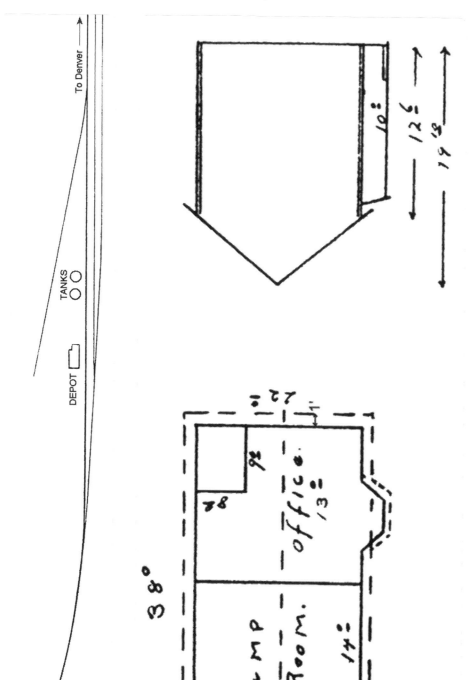

29

Beaver, CO

FIRST DEPOT

Built: 1885.
Construction: One-story
frame of 12' x 36', with 12' x 14' addition.
Moved to Portland 1904.

SECOND DEPOT

Built: 1910 by G. W. Myer.
Construction: One-story
frame of 20' x 57', with two 4' x 11' additions.
Roof: Hip, wood shingles.
Walls: Stucco with 3' drop siding wainscot.

Not in use by 1920.
Moved to Concrete by 1923.

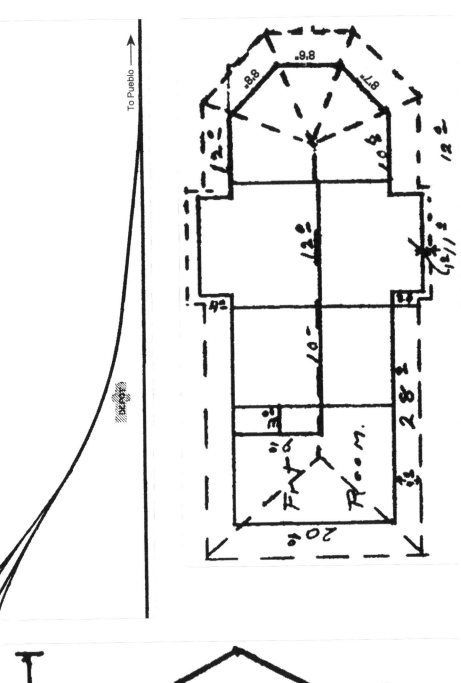

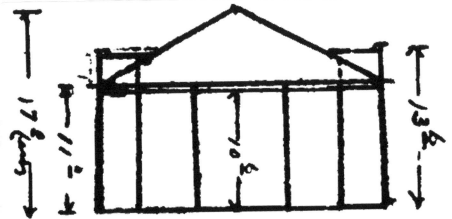

Concrete, CO

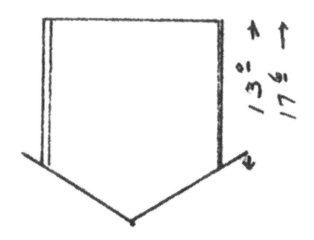

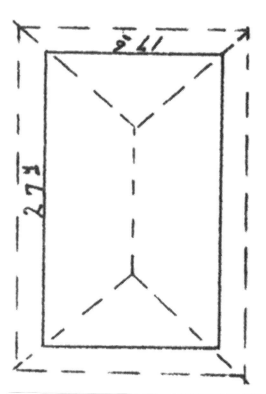

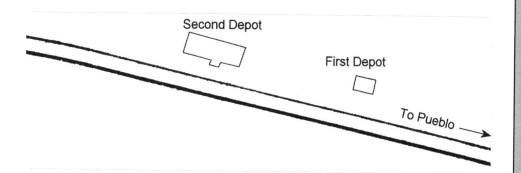

ELEVATION Not Available

FIRST DEPOT

Built: 1910.
Construction: One-story structure of 17'6" x 27'9".
Roof: Hip, wood shingles.
Walls: Concrete block.

Destroyed by flood in 1921.

SECOND DEPOT

Built: 1910.
Moved: From Beaver in 1923.
Construction: Two-story frame of 20' x 57' with two 4' x 11' additions.
(Please see Beaver depot for plan.)

Retired 1939.

Florence, CO

FIRST DEPOT

Built: 1890.
Construction: Two-story
frame structure of
24'4" x 99'3", with 3'6"
x 11'4" addition.
Roof: Gable, wood
shingles.
Walls: Lap siding with
3'6" beaded wainscot.

Remodeled to a freight
depot in 1918.
Office end retired 1924
and 24' x 48' balance
retired 1954.

SECOND DEPOT

Built: 1918.
Construction: One-story structure of 26' x
124', with 3 pavilions.
Roof: Hip, tiles.
Walls: Brick.

Retired 1968.

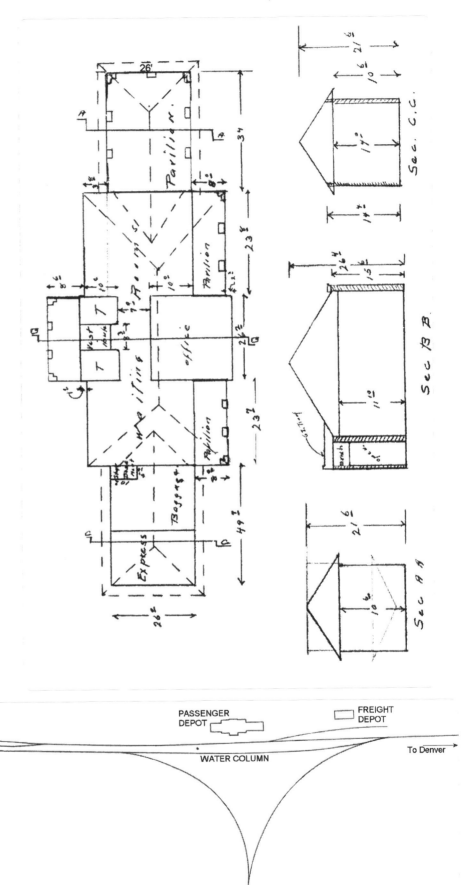

Canon City, CO

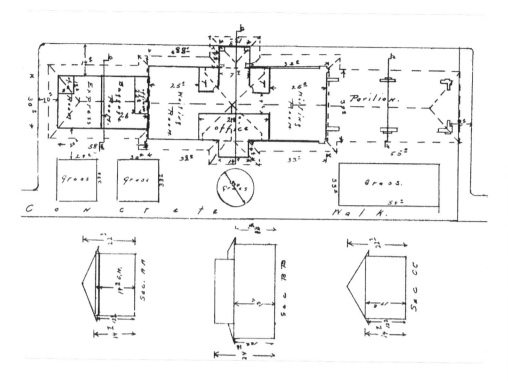

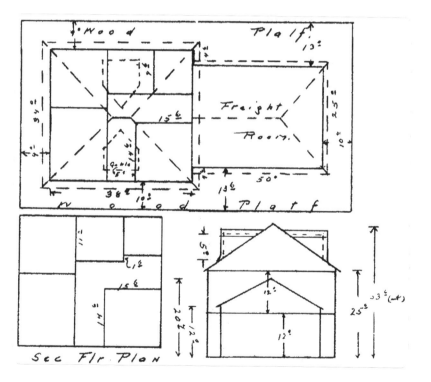

PASSENGER DEPOT

TANK

WATER COLUMN

FREIGHT DEPOT
1 BLOCK ——→

ELEVATION 5344'

FIRST DEPOT

Built by 1879.
Construction: One-story of 24' x 76', with 30' x '30' addition.
Roof: Gable, wood shingles.
Walls: Drop siding.

Moved and used as a freight house ~1911.

PASSENGER DEPOT

Built between 1909-10.
Construction: One-story structure of 40'X194'.
Roof: Hip, tiles.
Walls: Brick.

Retired 1968.

FIRST FREIGHT DEPOT

Built: 1902
Construction: One-story frame 36' x 62'.

Retired 1911 (sold and removed)

SECOND FREIGHT DEPOT

Construction: First depot used from c1911.

Retired 1956

33

Gorge, CO

DEPOT

Built: 1900.
Construction: One-story frame structure of 22' x 33'.
Roof: Hip, wood shakes.
Walls: Board and batten with 3' M & B wainscot.

Retired 1941.

To Pueblo

Depot

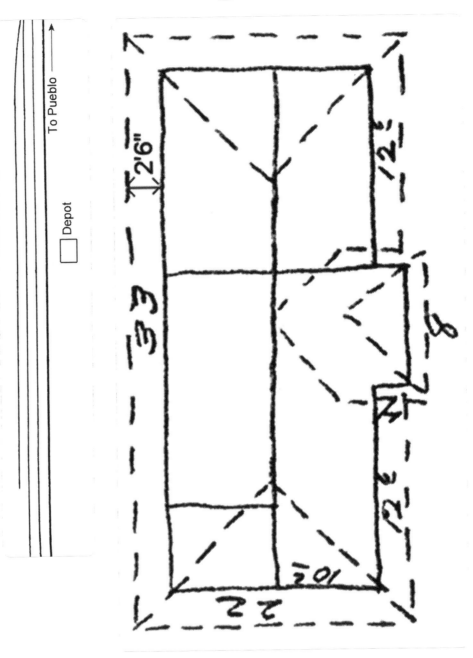

34

Parkdale, CO

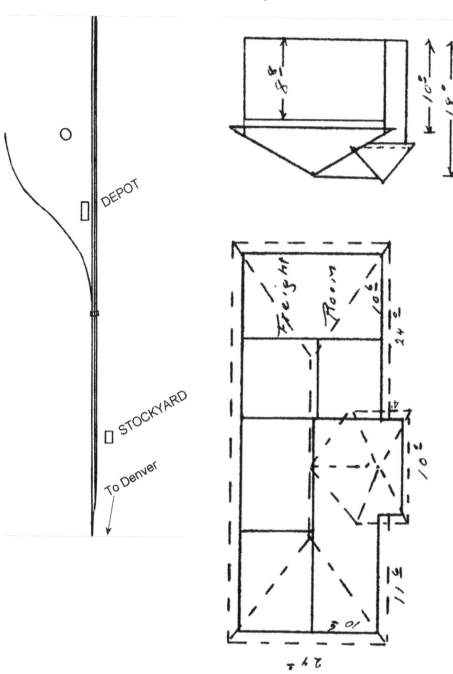

ELEVATION 5800'

PASSENGER DEPOT

Built: 1890.
Construction: One-story frame of 24' x 46', with a 4' x 10' addition.
Roof: Hip, wood shingles.
Walls: Board and batten with 4' beaded wainscot.

Retired 1970.

DEPOT

STOCKYARD

To Denver

Freight Room

35

DEPOT

Built: Not Available.
Construction: One-story frame structure of 18' x 30'.
Roof: Gable, wood shingles.
Walls: Board and batten.

Converted to section house by 1920.

Echo, CO

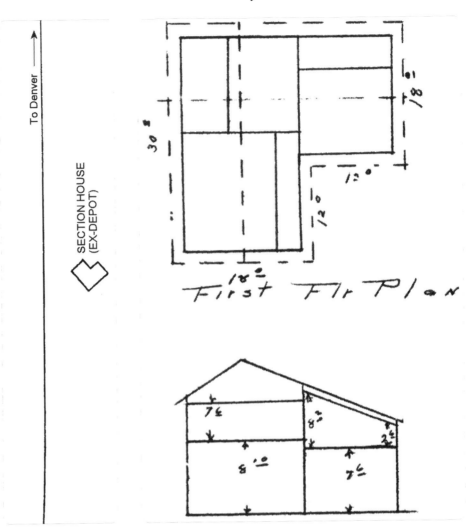

To Denver

SECTION HOUSE
(EX-DEPOT)

30⁸

18⁸

18⁸

12⁰

12⁰

First Flr Plan

7⁴

8²

2⁵

8'⁰

7⁵

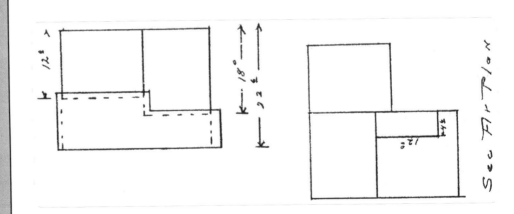

12⁸

18⁰

22⁶

3⁴

12⁸

Sec Flr Plan

Texas Creek, CO

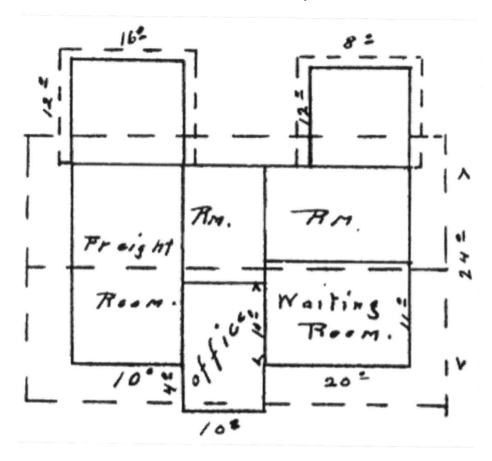

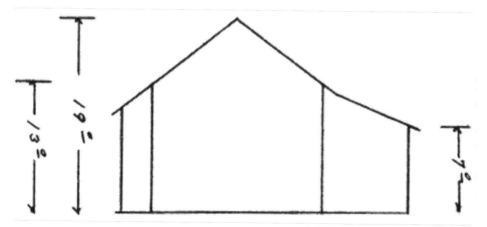

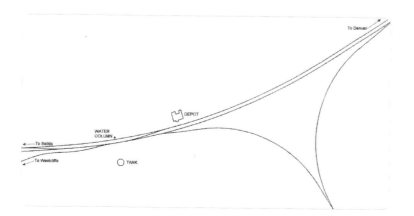

ELEVATION 6210'

DEPOT

Built: Not Available.
Construction: One-story frame structure of 24' x 40', with an 11' x 16' addition.
Roof: Gable, wood shingles.
Walls: Lap siding.

Retired 1970.

37

DEPOT

Built: Unlisted.
Construction: One-story frame structure of 24'x48' with 24'x48' (Freight). With 12'x20', 4'x12', 12'x16' and 4'x16' (Porch) additions.
Roof: Hip, wood shingles.
Walls: Board and batten.

Retired 1956.

Cotopaxi, CO

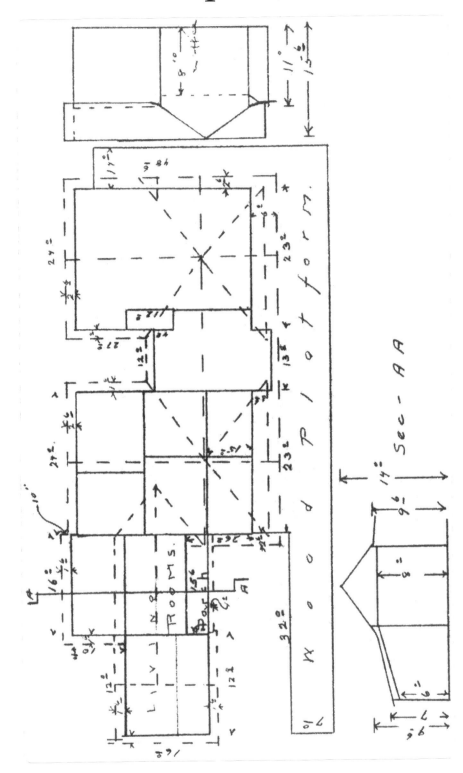

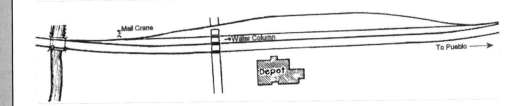

Howard, CO

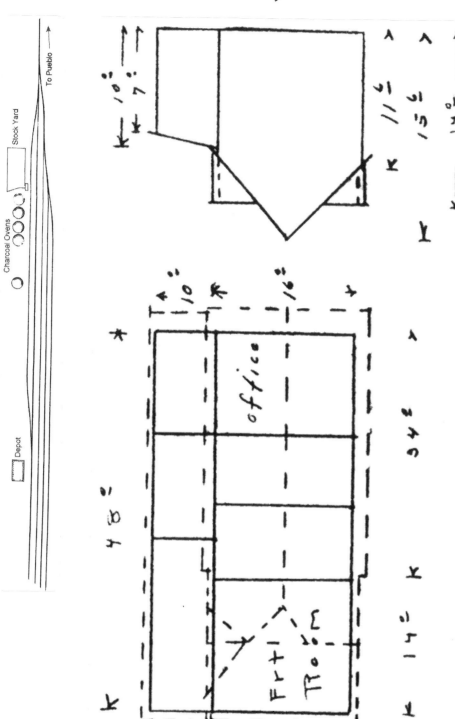

39

Welsville, CO

ELEVATION: ~6900'

DEPOT

Built: 1890.
Construction: One-story frame structure of 16' x 24'.

Retired by 1900.

Otis, CO

ELEVATION: Not Available

DEPOT

Built: 1890.
Construction: One-story frame structure of 16' x 24'.

Retired. Taken down in 1912 as it was not used for a number of years.

Salida, CO 1-2

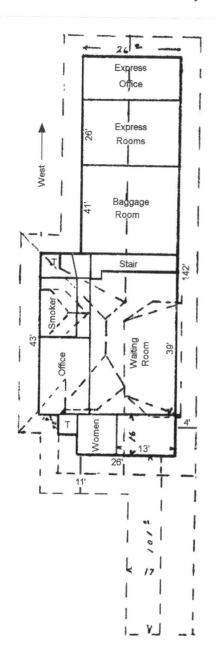

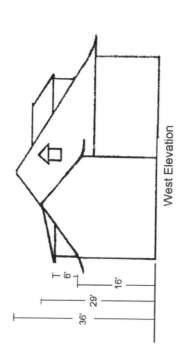

West Elevation

ELEVATION 7050'

FIRST PASSENGER DEPOT

Built: 1880.
Construction: One-story structure of 40' x 43'. Additions of 15' x 26', 26' x 42' and 6' x 6'.
Addition of 26' x 40' in 1913.
Roof: Gable, wood shingles except west 40' composition No.2.
Walls: Stone.

Retired 1942.

SECOND PASSENGER DEPOT

Built: 1942.
Construction: Two-story structure. Art-deco style. Dimensions not available.
Different location from first depot.

Retired 1985.

FREIGHT DEPOT

Built: 1891.
Construction: Frame structure of 20' x 51'.
Roof: Wood shingles.
Walls: Drop siding with 3' beaded wainscot.
Enlarged to 20' x 65', in 1920.

Destroyed by fire October 23 1926.
Removed 1927.
Replaced by steel structure of 24' x 80' on a different site.
Extended by 20' x 24' 1948.

Sold 1961 to D&RG Motor Way.
Retired 1990.

Salida, CO 2-2

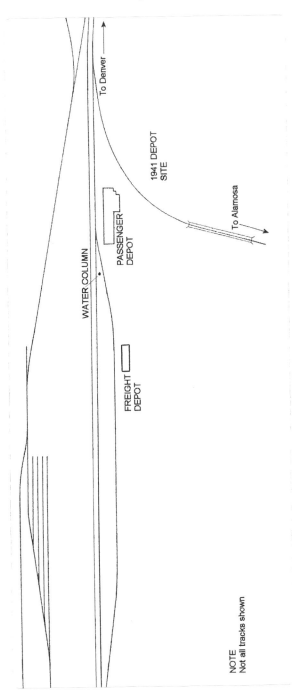

To Denver

1941 DEPOT SITE

To Alamosa

WATER COLUMN

PASSENGER DEPOT

FREIGHT DEPOT

NOTE
Not all tracks shown

Photos 1

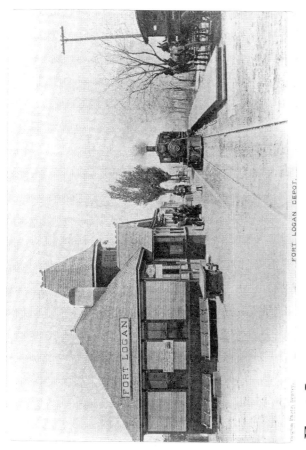

Fort Logan ↗
Louviers ↘

Littleton ↗
Sedalia ↘

43

Photos 2

Castle Rock ↗
Palmer Lake ↘

Larkspur ↗
Monument ↘

Photos 3

Colorado Springs ↗

Wigwam ↗

Fountain ↗

Pueblo Union ↗

Photos 4

Canon City ↗

Texas Creek ↘

Gorge ↗

Photos 5

Salida (reverse) ↗

Salida(1967) ↗

Salida ↗

47

BROWN CANON TO GRAND JUNCTION

Miles from Denver
to:

Brown Canon	222.23	Gypsum	335.83
Nathrop	232.83	Shoshone	350.50
Buena Vista	240.32	Glenwod Springs	360.09
Riverside	240.86	Newcastle	372.67
Yale (ex-Granite)	257.31	Silt	379.45
Malta	271	Antlers	382.31
Leadville	275.82	Rifle	386.65
Tennessee Pass	280.99	Morris	395.33
Pando	288.53	Grand Valley	403.97
Red Cliff	293.94	DeBeque	416.60
Minturn	301.95	Palisade	437.07
Avon	307.94	Clifton	442.59
Wolcott	319.05	Grand Junction	449.56
Eagle	328.98		

Brown Canon, CO

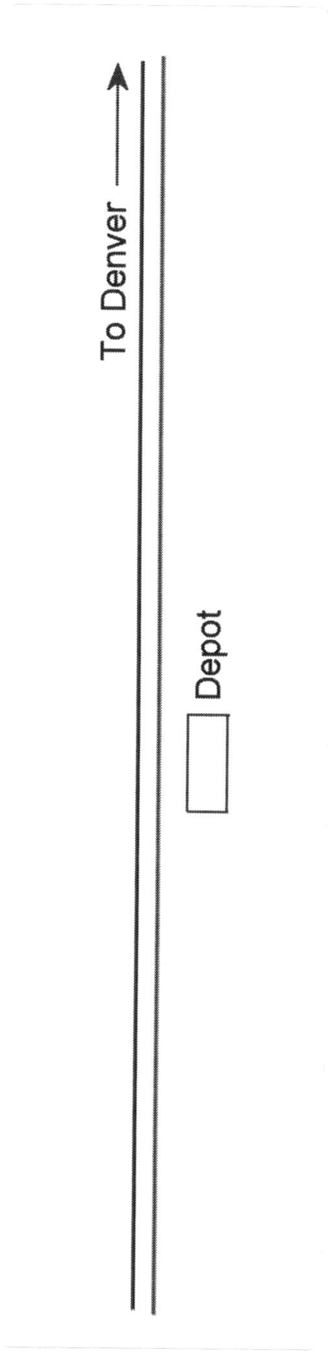

To Denver →

Depot

DEPOT

Built: 1885.
Construction: One-story frame structure of 12' x 18'.
Roof: Gable, wood shingles.
Walls: Board and batten.

Assigned to section workers by 1920. No depot plan available.

Retired in 1962.

Nathrop, CO

DEPOT

Built: 1880.
Construction: One-story structure of 26' x 60'.
Roof: Hip, corrugated iron.
Wood: Shingles by 1920.
Walls: Rubble stone in mortar.

Not in use by 1920.
Retired 1947.

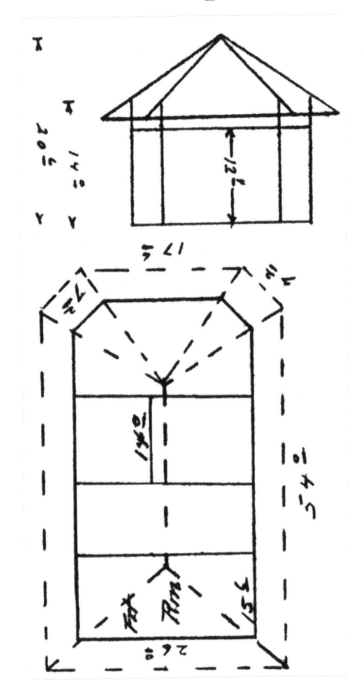

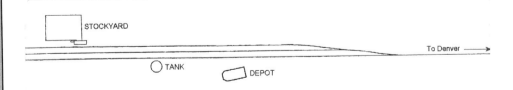

STOCKYARD

TANK   DEPOT   To Denver →

Buena Vista, CO

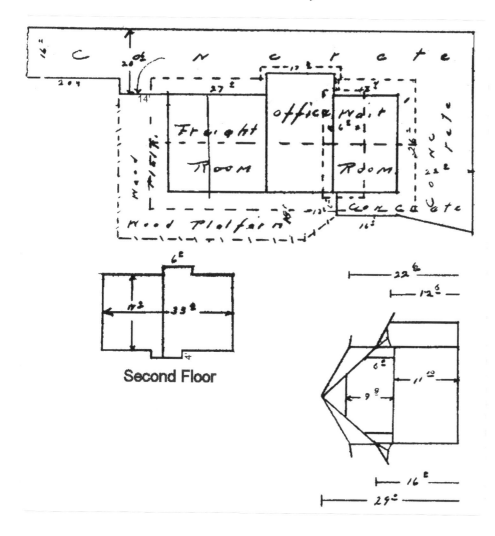

Second Floor

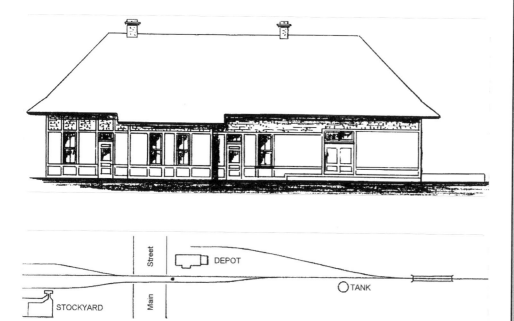

FIRST DEPOT

Built: 1890. According to Bridges & Buildings book.
Construction: One & two-story frame structure of 26' x 57'.
Roof: Hip, wood shingles.
Walls: Board and batten.

Damaged by fire and remodeled in 1925.
Retired 1948.

SECOND DEPOT

Built: 1948.
Construction: One-story brick structure 21' x 45', with operator's bay 3' x 10'8" and flat roof.

Retired 1968.

Riverside, CO

DEPOT

Built: 1880.
Construction: One-story frame of 16' x 24', with a 12' x 13' addition.
Roof: Gable, wood shingles.
Walls: Board and batten.

Used as a section house by 1920.
Retired 1947.

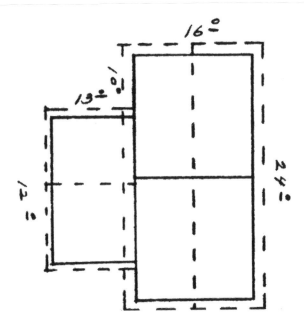

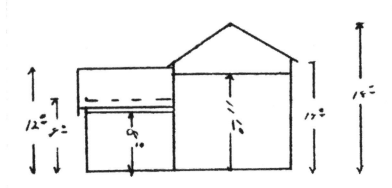

DEPOT

To Denver ⟶

Granite(Yale),CO

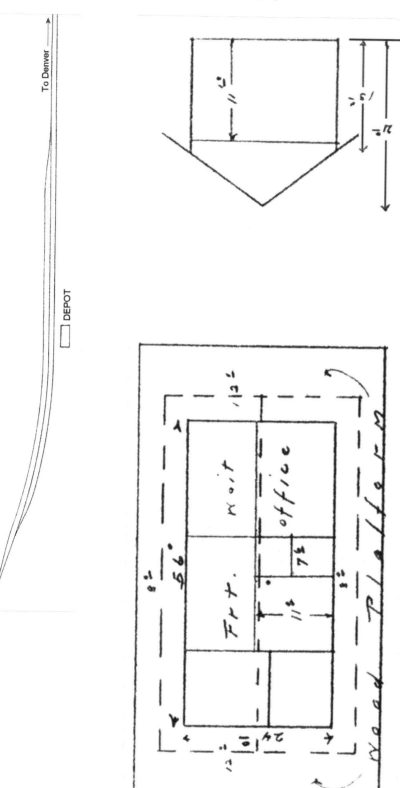

To Denver

DEPOT

Wait

office

Frt.

Wood Platform

ELEVATION 8943'

DEPOT

Built: 1884.
Construction: One-story frame structure of 24' x 56'.
Roof: Gable, wood shingles.
Walls: Board and batten.
Retired 1963.

Malta, CO

DEPOT

Built: 1893.
Construction: One-story frame structure of 20' x 40'x 20' x 53'.
Roof: Gable, wood shingles.
Walls: Board and batten with 4' beaded wainscot.

Retired 1962.
Replaced with metal shelter, which was retired 1980.

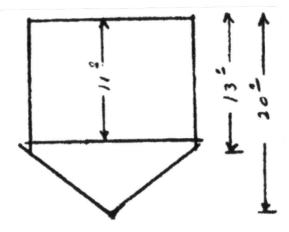

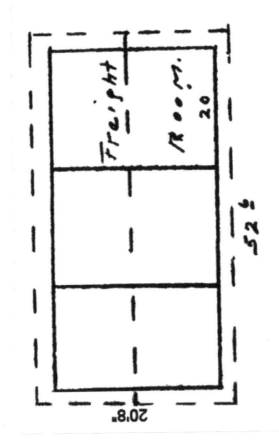

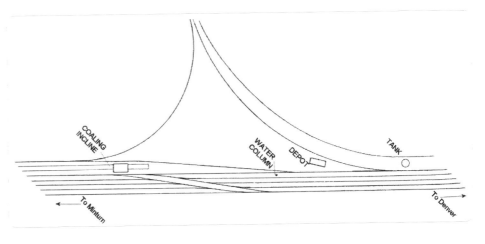

Leadville, CO

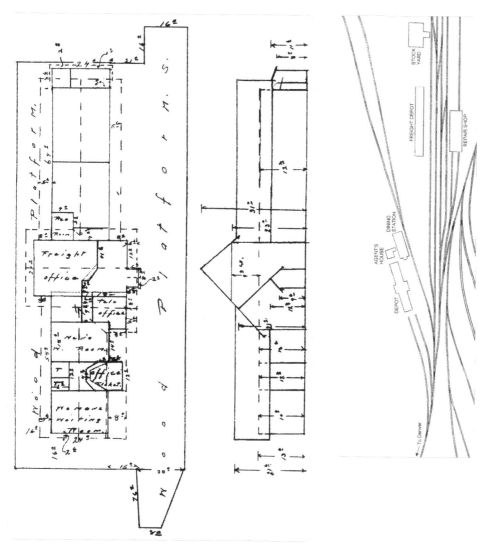

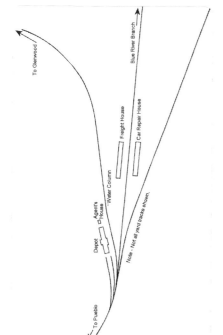

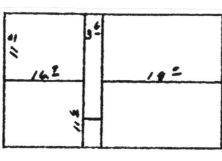

Sec Flr Plan.

ELEVATION 10200'

PASSENGER DEPOT

Built: By 1883.
Construction: Two story frame structure of 24' x 40'. One-story additions of 24' x 58' and 24' x 64'; waiting room end extended 20'.
Roof: Gable, wood shingles.
Walls: Lap siding with second floor wood shakes.

Remodeled 1900. Retired in 1940 and replaced by freight depot.

FREIGHT DEPOT

Built: By 1890.
Construction: Frame structure of 24' x 200'.
Roof: Wood shingles.
Walls: Lap siding.
Remodeled in 1940 as passenger and freight depot.

Retired 1984.

ELEVATION 10242'

DEPOT

Built: 1890.
Construction: One-story frame structure of 24' x 33'.
Roof: Hip, wood shingles.
Walls: Board and batten.

Retired 1961.

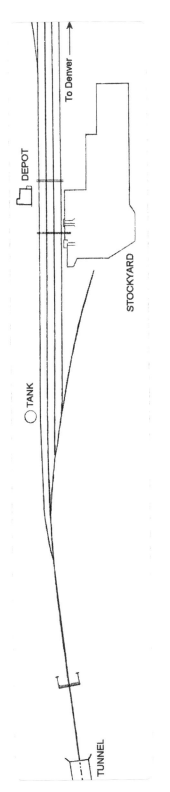

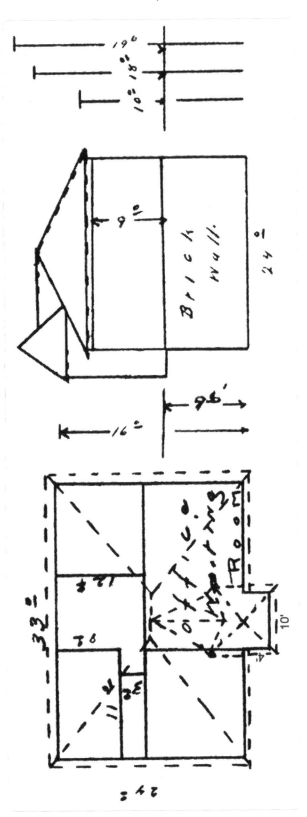

Pando, CO

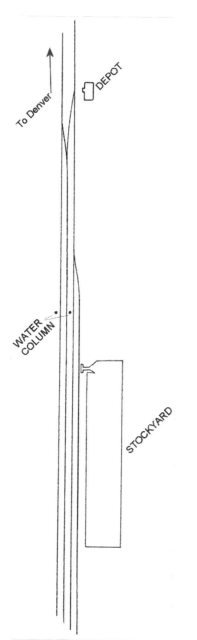

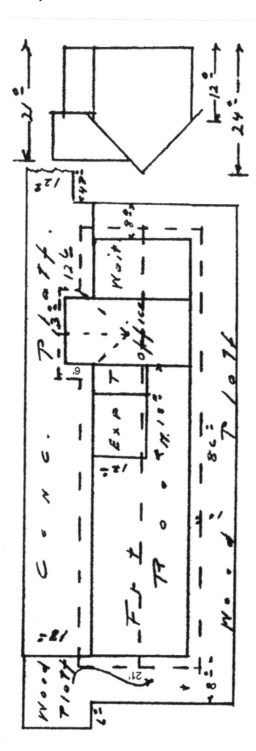

Red Cliff, CO

DEPOT

Built in 1890.
Construction: One-story frame structure of 24' x 100' with a 4' x 12' bay window addition.
Roof: Gable, wood shingles.
Walls: Lap siding.

Retired in 1948.

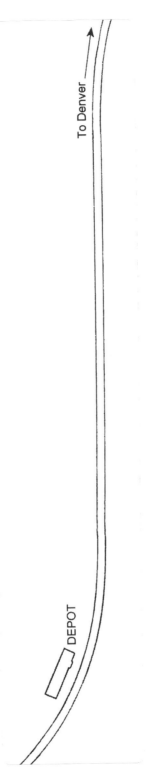

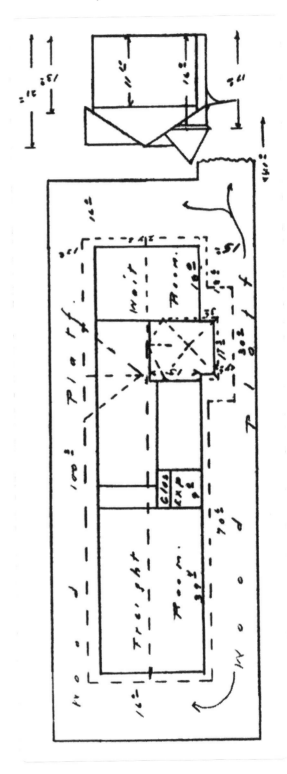

Minturn, CO

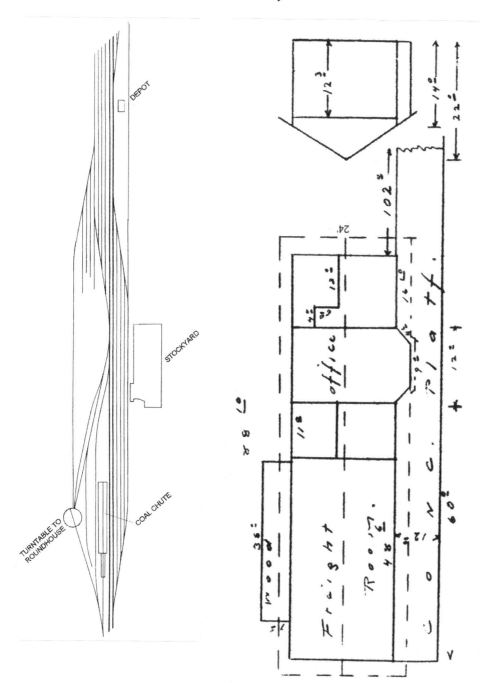

Avon, CO

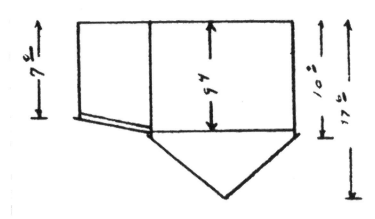

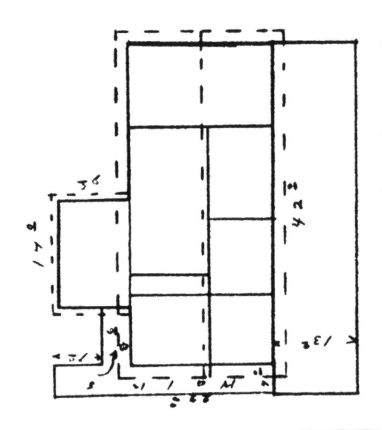

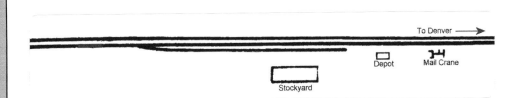

Depot

Mail Crane

Stockyard

To Denver →

ELEVATION 7465'

DEPOT

Built: 1900.
Construction: One-story frame 22' x 30'.
Addition of 22' x 12' in 1907.
Roof - Gable, wood shingles.
Walls - Board & batten.

Retired 1959

Wolcott, CO

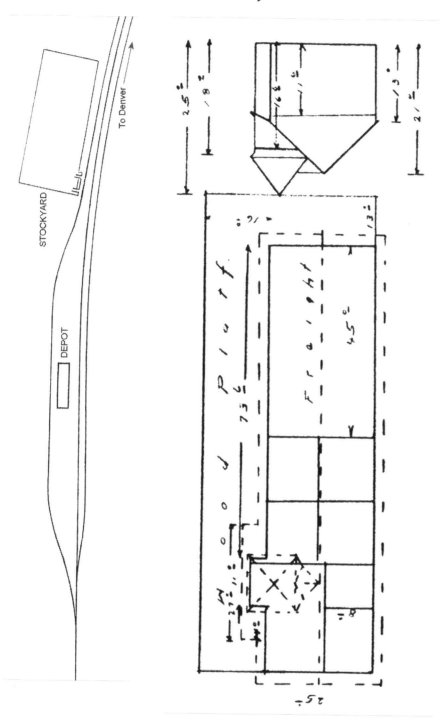

ELEVATION 6976'

DEPOT

Built:1890.
Construction: One-story frame 25' x 67', Additions of 25'x 32' and 4' x 12'.
Roof: Gable, wood shingles.
Walls: Lap siding with 3' beaded wainscot.

Retired 1963.

61

Eagle, CO

DEPOT

Built: 1900.
Construction: One-story frame structure of 24' x 63', with 4' x 10' bay.
Roof: Gable. Hip from 1949; wood shingles.
Walls: Board and batten. Lap siding from 1949.

Modernized in 1949. Retired 1968.

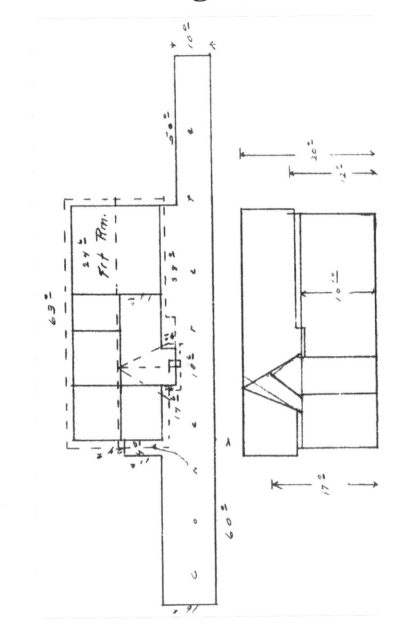

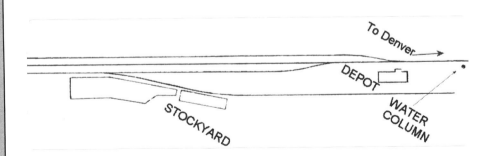

Gypsum, CO

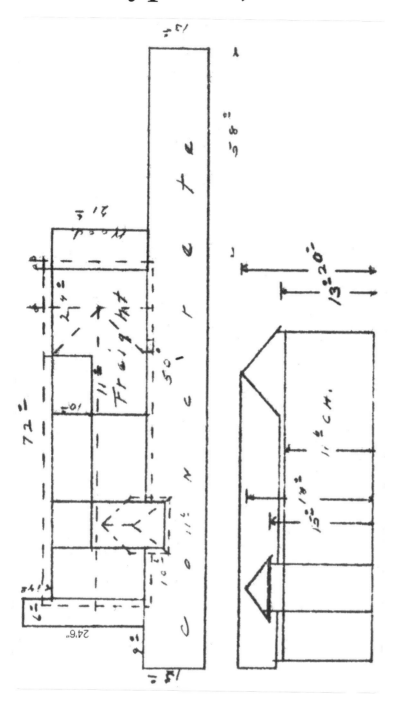

DEPOT

STOCKYARD

DEPOT

Built: 1889.
Construction: One-story frame structure 22' x 47'. Extended in 1891 by 4' x 12'. addition and 1907 to 22' x 67'.
Roof: Gable, wood shingles.
Walls: Board and batten.

Retired 1970.

Shoshone, CO

DEPOT

Built: 1901.
Construction: One-story frame structure of 24' x 34'.
Roof: Hip, wood shingles.
Walls: Wood shingles with 4' board and batten wainscot.

Retired 1967

FREIGHT HOUSE
Added: Not available
Construction: Car body

Retired 1939.

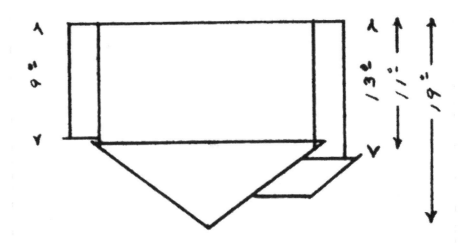

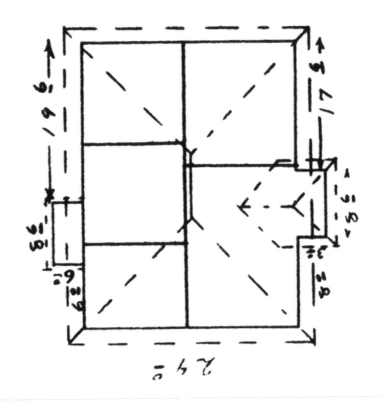

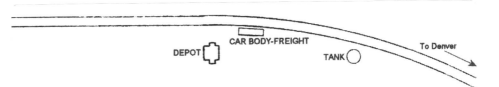

DEPOT   CAR BODY-FREIGHT   TANK   To Denver

Glenwood Springs, CO

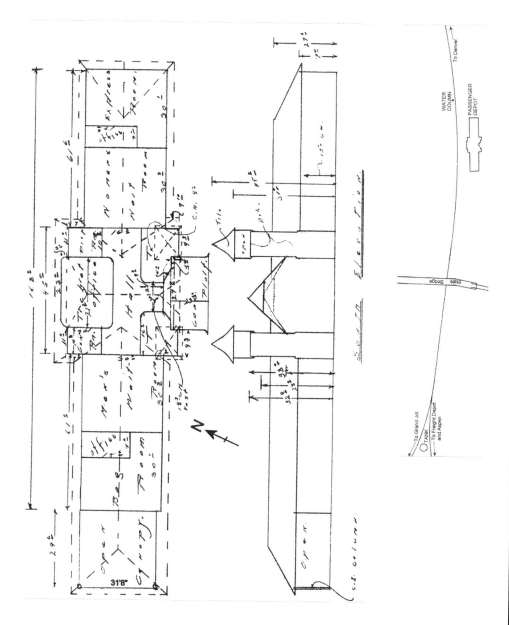

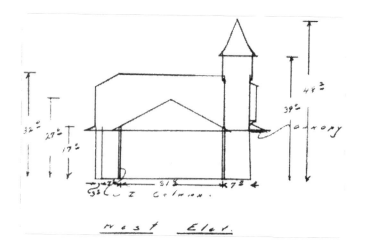

ELEVATION 5562'

DEPOT

Built: By 1893.
Construction: Frame
22' x 90'.
(No details available)

Depot purchased from
Colorado Midland RR.
1921.

66

Newcastle, CO

To Denver ⟶

DEPOT

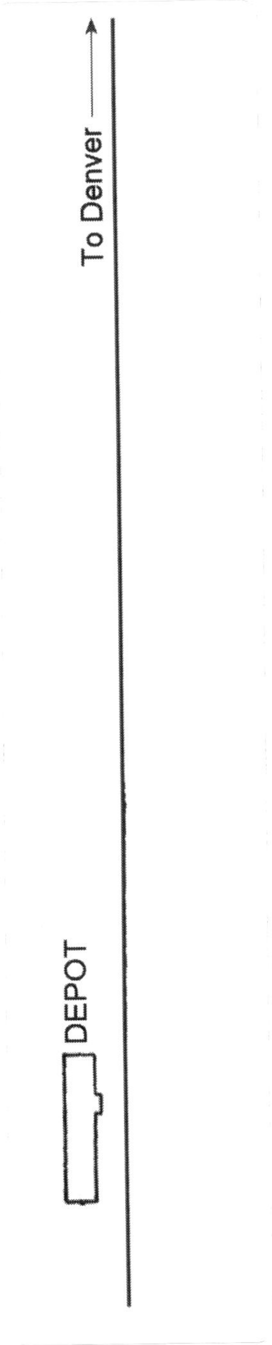

Silt, CO

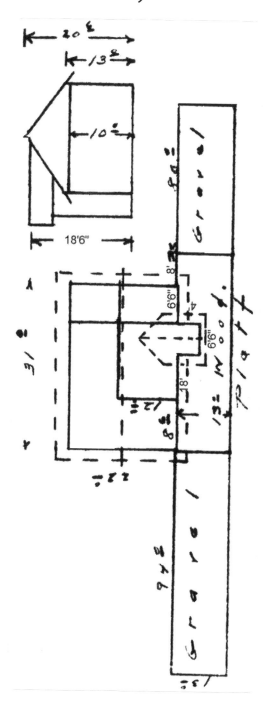

18'6"

MAIL
CRANE

DEPOT

To Denver →

ELEVATION 5441'

DEPOT

Built: Not Available
Construction: One-
story frame structure
of 22' x 31'.
Roof: Gable, wood
shingles.
Walls: Board and
batten.
Enlarged in 1920 to
provide a 16' x 22'
freight and baggage
room and 4'6" x 22'.
waiting room.
Remodeled and size
reduced 1950.

Retired 1966.

ELEVATION 5432'

DEPOT

Built: Not Available.
Construction: One-
story frame of 14' x 16'.
Roof: Gable, wood
shingles.
Walls: Lap siding.

Retired 1941.

68

Antlers, CO

To Denver

DEPOT

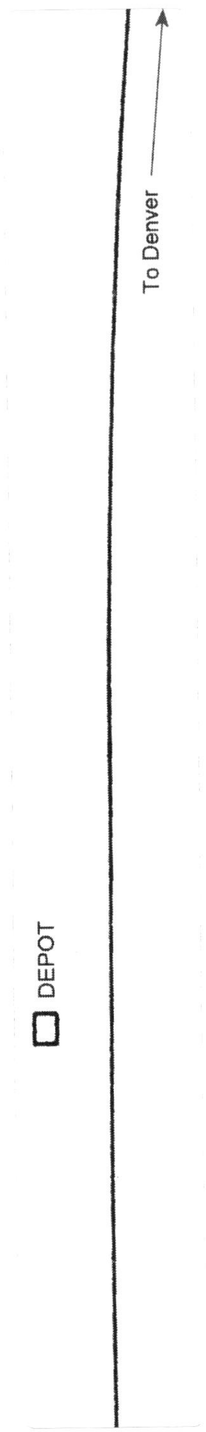

Rifle, CO

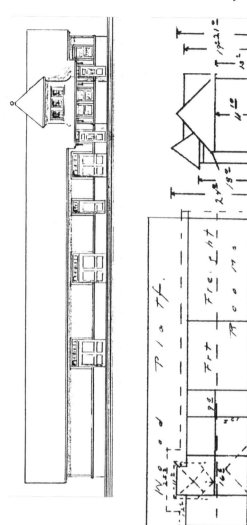

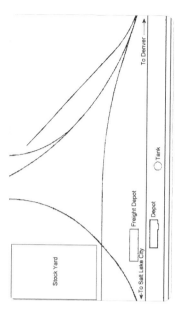

DEPOT

Built: 1890.
Construction: One-story frame structure of 24' x 82'. Freight room extended 30' by 1920.
Roof: Gable, wood shingles.
Walls: Lap siding.

Rebuilt in 1924 with separate freight and passenger buildings; this provided a 24' x 88' freight depot.

Rebuilt in 1949 with a flat roof.

Retired 1966.
Closed as agency station 1972.

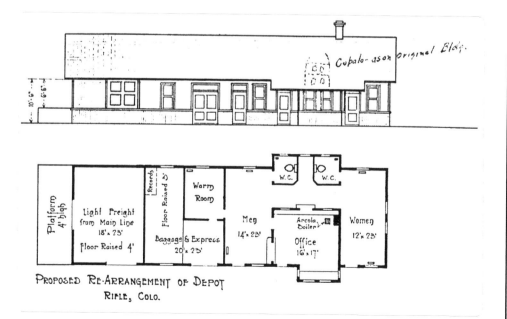

PROPOSED RE-ARRANGEMENT OF DEPOT
RIFLE, COLO.

Morris, CO

DEPOT

Built: Not Available.
Construction: One-story frame structure of 22' x 30'.
Roof: Gable, wood shingles.
Walls: Board and batten.

Retired 1939.

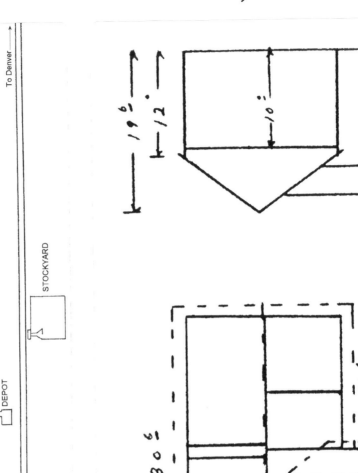

To Denver

STOCKYARD

DEPOT

Grand Valley, CO

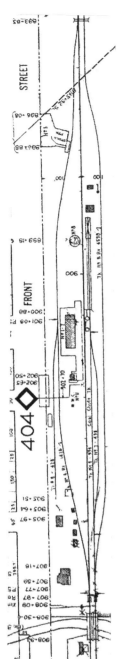

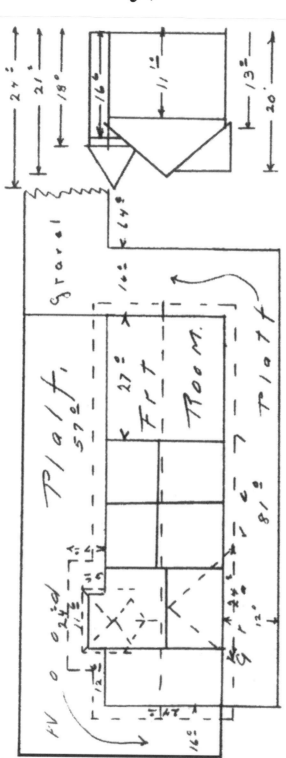

ELEVATION 5104'

DEPOT

Built: Not Available.
Construction: One-story frame structure of 24' x 81'.
Roof: Gable, wood shingles.
Walls: Lap siding with 3'6" beaded wainscot.

Modernized in 1948.
Retired 1968.

De Beque, CO

ELEVATION 4945'

DEPOT

Built: Not Available.
Construction: One-story frame structure of 24' x 81'.
(Same as Grand Valley depot.)
Roof: Gable, wood shingles.
Walls: Lap siding with 3'6" beaded wainscot.

Modernized in 1948. Shortened to 61'6" and bay window removed.

Retired 1970.

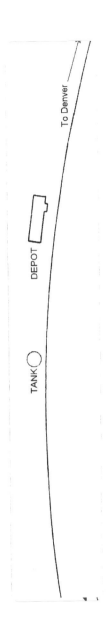

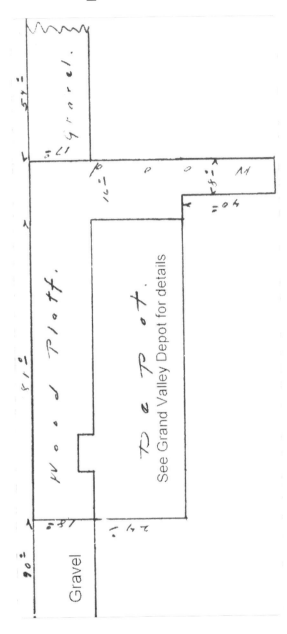

Wood Platt.

Depot
See Grand Valley Depot for details

Gravel

Palisade, CO

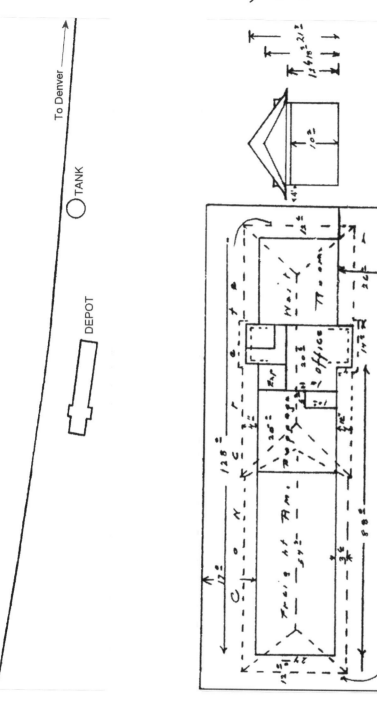

ELEVATION 4741'

<u>DEPOT</u>   **73**

Built: 1909.
Construction: One-
story structure of 24' x
128'.
Roof: Hip, tile.
Walls: Stucco finish.

Retired 1972.

Clifton, CO

DEPOT

Built: 1909.
Construction: One-story frame structure of 22' x 63'.
Roof: Hip, wood shingles. Changed later to tiles.
Walls: Stucco with 3' drop siding wainscot.

Retired 1962.

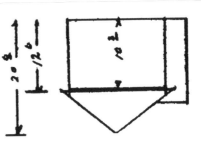

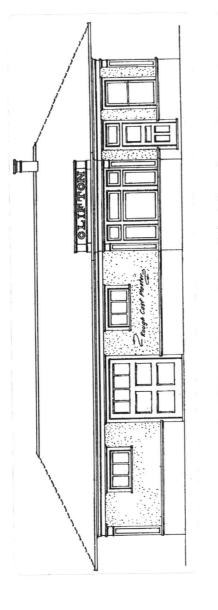

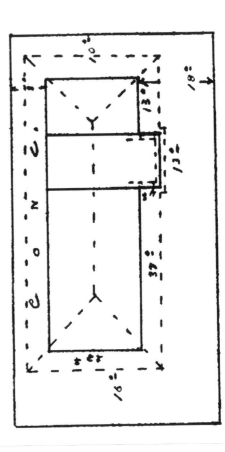

☐ DEPOT   To Denver ⟶

Grand Junction, CO

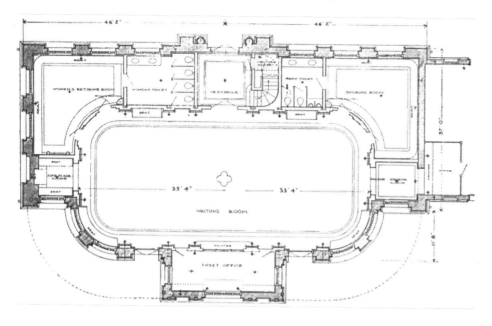

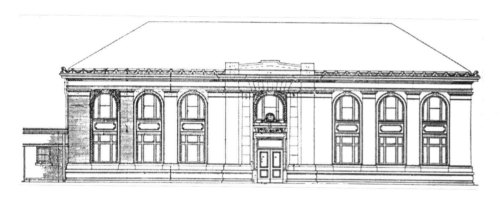

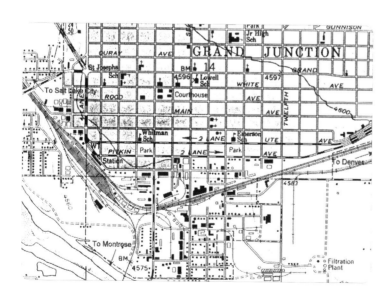

FIRST DEPOT
Built: Not Available.
Construction: One-story frame structure of 30' x 30'. With 10' x 28', 28' x 86' and 2' x 14' additions.

Retired in 1906
Torn down in 1909.

SECOND DEPOT
Built: 1906
Construction: Two-story brick structure 48' x 92'.

FREIGHT DEPOT 1
Built: 1906
Construction: Frame structure of 20' x 175'
Roof: Composition.

Destroyed by fire September 22 1918. Replaced 1920 by brick 2-story 37' x 64'.

FREIGHT DEPOT 2
Built: 1919.
Construction: Structure of two-story 37' x 64 'office and one-story 36' x 181' freight room.
Roof: Gable, tile.
Walls: Brick.

Extended by 36' x 80' 1941.
Retired 1966.

Photos 6

Yale ↗
Leadville ↗

Buena Vista ↗
Malta ↗

Photos 7

Pando ↗
Minturn ↘

Tennessee Pass ↗
Red Cliff ↘

Photos 8

Wolcott ↗
Gypsum ↗

Avon ↗
Eagle ↗

Photos 9

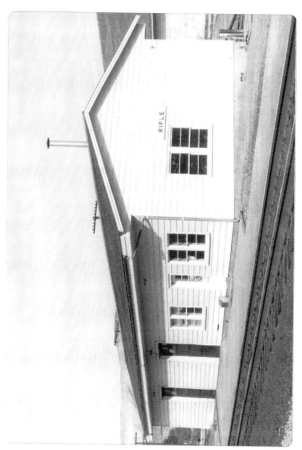

Newcastle ↗
Rifle ↘

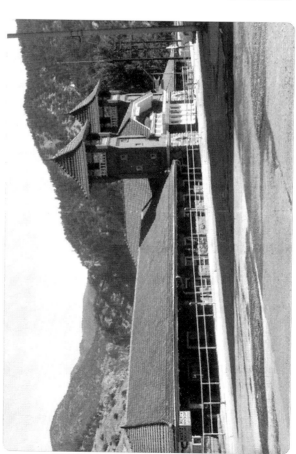

Shoshone ↗
Glenwood Springs ↗

79

De Beque ↗

Grand Junction ↗

Grand Valley ↗

Clifton ↘

MINNEQUA TO TRINIDAD

Miles from Denver
to:

Minnequa.............. 121.42	Rouse Junction...... 175.63
Marnell................. 133.60	Augusta................. 188.81
Cedarwood........... 142.03	Barnes.................. 192.32
Walsenburg........... 170.44	Chicosa................. 196.26
Sandy................... 164.12	El Moro................. 203.99
Huerfano.............. 156.74	Trinidad................ 208.27
Cuchara Junction.. 166.73	

Minnequa, CO

FIRST DEPOT

Built: 1883.
Construction: One-story frame 18' x 50', with a 4' x 12' addition.
Destroyed by fire October 28 1901.

SECOND DEPOT

Built: 1902.
Construction: One-story brick 24' x 78', with a 4' x 18' bay window.
Roof: Hip, tile.
Walls: Brick.

Retired 1956.
Modern structure added in 1978.

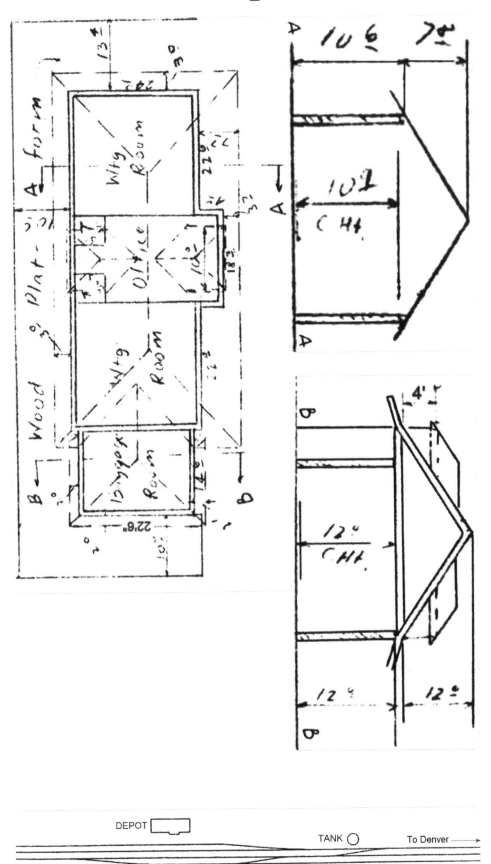

DEPOT

TANK

To Denver

Marnell, CO

ELEVATION 5130'

DEPOT

Built: 1911.
Construction: One-story frame structure. Officially described as
Type IV.

Retired 1960.

Cedarwood, CO

ELEVATION 5606'

DEPOT

Built: 1911.
Construction: One-story frame structure. Officially described as
Type IV.

Retired 1967.

Walsenburg, CO

FIRST DEPOT

Built: Not Available.
Construction: One-story frame structure of 16' x 64'.

Replaced 1891.

SECOND DEPOT

Built: 1891.
Construction: One-story frame structure of 24' x 134', with additions of 4' x 12' and 5' x 24'.
Roof: Gable, wood shingles.
Walls: Lap siding with 4' M&B wainscot.

Destroyed by fire c1927.

THIRD DEPOT

Built: 1927.
Construction: Brick passenger depot jointly owned by D&RG and C&S. Separate freight house approx.30' x 115'.

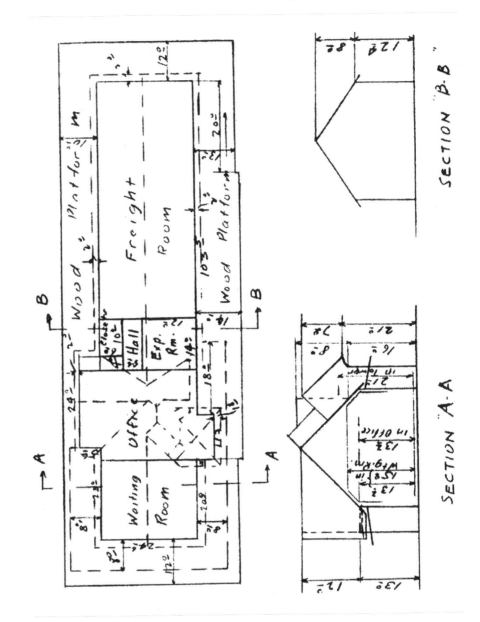

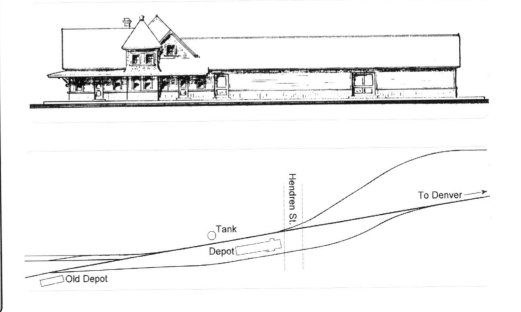

Sandy, CO

ELEVATION: 6007'

<u>DEPOT</u>

Built: 1911.
Construction: One-story frame structure of 22' x 50'. Officially described as Type IV.

Retired 1946.

Huerfano, CO

ELEVATION 5677'

DEPOT

Built: 1889.
Construction: One-story frame structure of 21' x 55' (7 rooms), with 4' x 11' addition. (No plan of depot available).

Sold and removed 1917.
Replaced by car body.

Retired 1932.

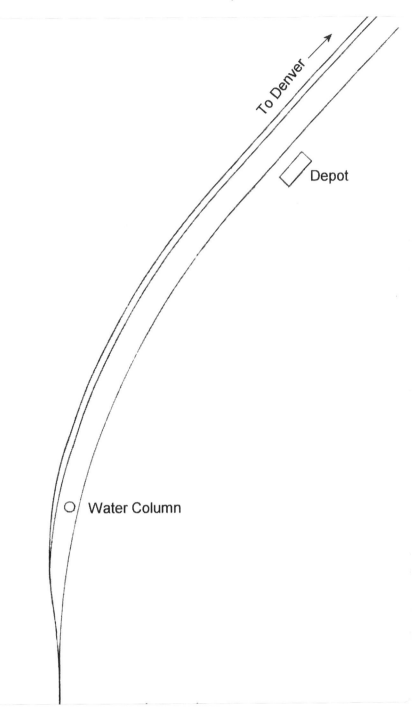

To Denver

Depot

Water Column

Cuchara Junction, CO

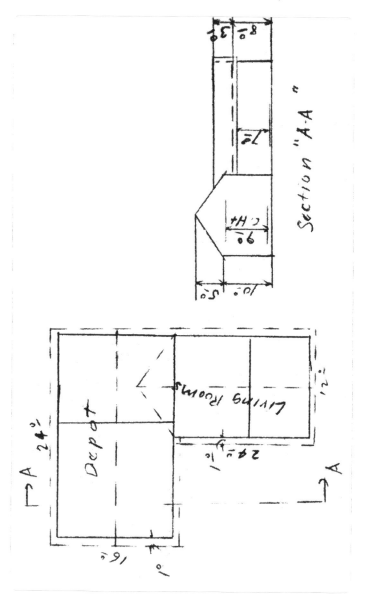

Section "A-A"

Depot

Living Rooms

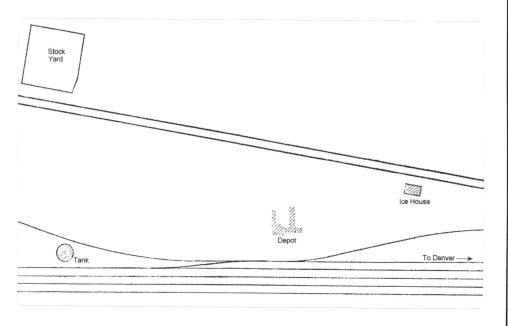

Stock Yard

Ice House

Depot

Tank

To Denver →

DEPOT

Built: 1889.
Construction: One-story frame structure of 24' x 74', with 3'5" x 9' and 14' x 30' additions.
Roof: Gable, wood shingles.
Walls: Board and batten.

Fire damaged August 29 1912.
Two 9' x 32' car bodies added to replace damaged portion. Shown in the track plan forming an inverted "T".

Destroyed by fire 1926.

DEPOT

Built: 1889.
Construction: One-story frame structure of 24' x 60', with a 4' x 11' addition.
Roof: Hip, wood shingles.
Walls: Lap siding with 3'8" beaded wainscot and 1 belt of wood shingles 2'6" deep. Upper 6' of bay wood shingles.

Retired 1936.

Rouse Junction, CO

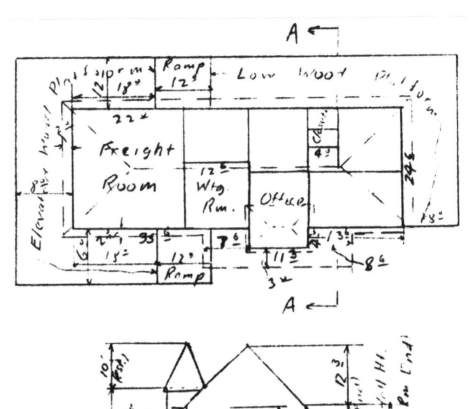

SECTION A-A

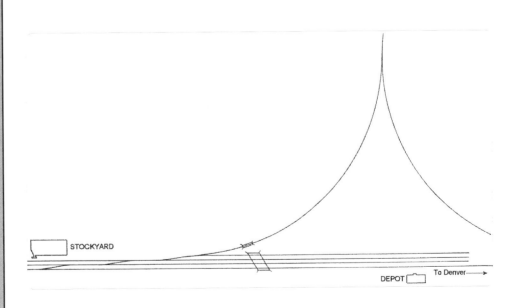

STOCKYARD

DEPOT   To Denver →

Augusta, CO

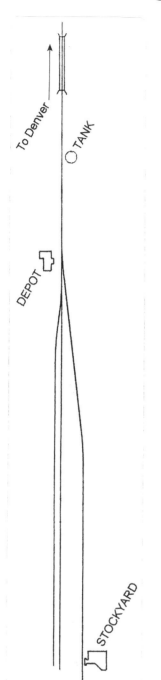

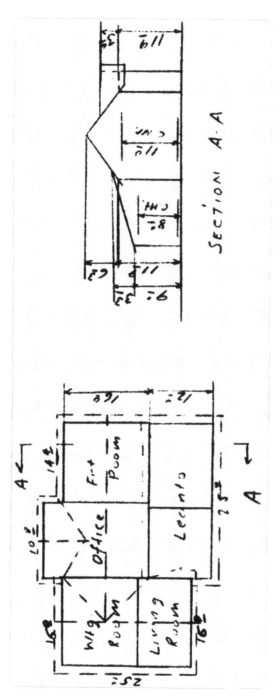

FIRST DEPOT

Built: 1883.
Construction: One-story frame of 16' x 50'.
Roof: Hip.
Walls: Drop siding with 3' beaded wainscot.

Moved to Barnes CO 1907.

SECOND DEPOT

Built: 1912.
Moved: Section houses from Salt Creek.
Construction: Two frame structures of 16' x 25'.
Roof: Gable, wood shingles.
Walls: Board and batten.

Lean-to added 1919.
Retired 1936.

DEPOT

Moved: from Augusta 1907.
One & Two-story frame structure of 16' x 50'.
Roof: Hip, metal shingles.
Walls: Drop siding with 3' M&B beaded wainscot.

Destroyed by fire September 22 1926. Replaced by car body for passenger depot.

Barnes, CO

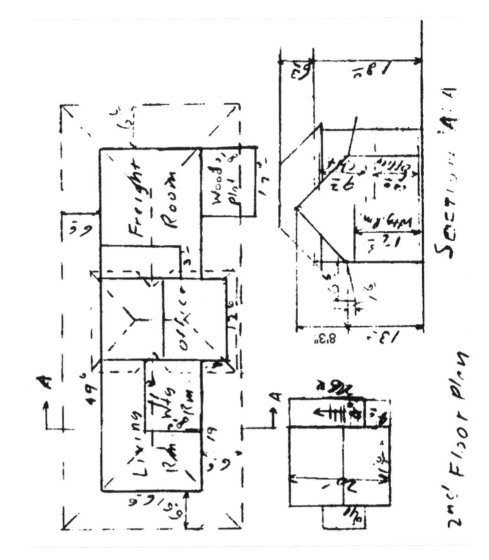

DEPOT

To Denver →

Chicosa, CO

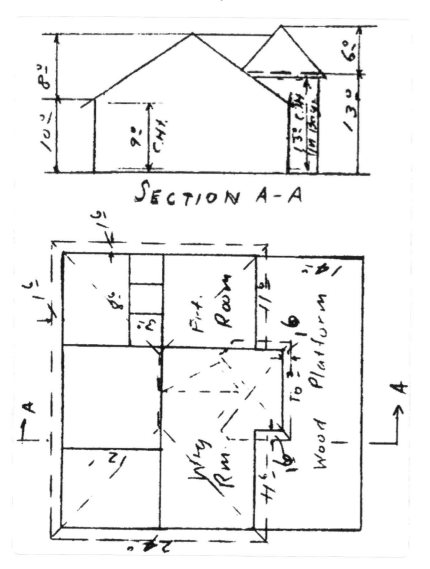

SECTION A-A

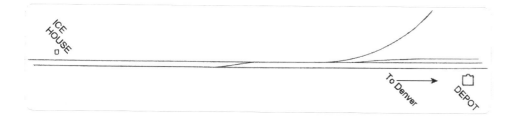

ICE HOUSE

To Denver →

DEPOT

ELEVATION 6116'

DEPOT

Built: 1890.
Construction: One-story frame structure of 24' x 33', with 4' x 10' addition.
Roof: Hip, wood shingles.
Walls: Board and batten with 4' M&B wainscot.

Retired 1936.

ELEVATION 5879'

FIRST DEPOT

Built: 1890.
Construction: One-story frame structure of 30' x 100'.

Destroyed by fire c1896.

SECOND DEPOT

Built:1896
Construction: One-story frame structure of 20' x 57', with a 3' x 12' addition.
(No plan available)

Destroyed by fire in 1910.

El Moro, CO

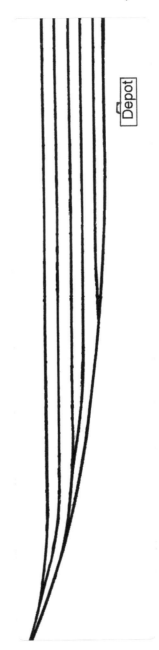

Depot

Trinidad, CO

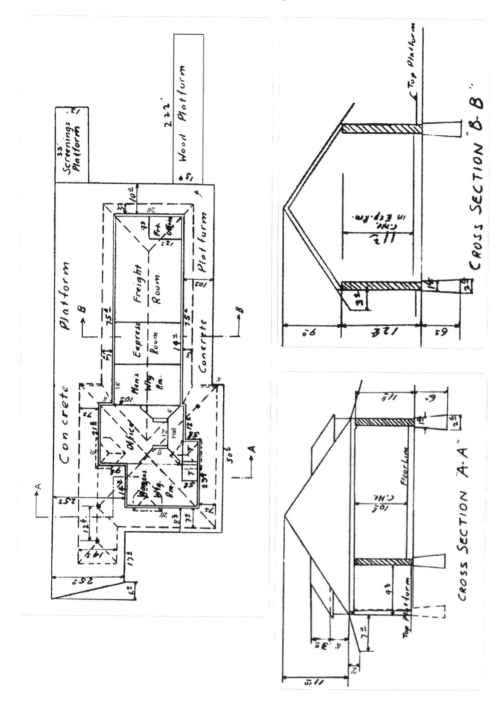

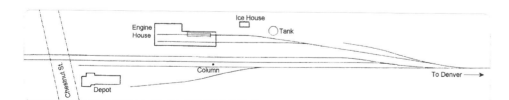

FIRST DEPOT

Built 1888.
Construction: One-story frame structure of 24' x 120'.

Retired 1901.

SECOND DEPOT

Built 1901.
Construction: One-story brick structure of 24' x 75', with additions of 21' x 28', 14' x 26' and 6' x 8'.
Roof: Hip, tile.
Walls: Brick.

Retired 1967.

Photos 11

Walsenberg

PONCHA JUCTION TO GUNNISON

Miles from Denver
to:

Poncha Junction..... 220.10

Maysville................ 227.01

Garfield................. 232.99

Monarch................. 235.40

Marshall Pass.......... 240.71

Sargent....... 257.24

Doyle.......... 269.46

Parlin.......... 276.82

Gunnison.... 288.64

Poncha Junction, CO

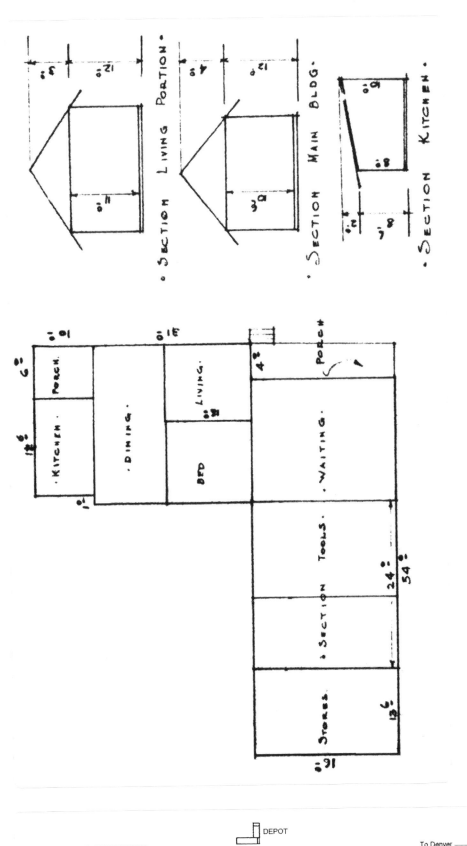

ELEVATION 7480'

DEPOT

Built: 1881.
Construction: One-story frame structure of 16' x 54' depot and section house, with a 18' x 31' addition.
Roof: Gable, and wood shingles.
Walls: Board and batten.

Replaced by a metal tool shed from Farmington CO (applies to Gato).
Retired 1964.

96

Maysville, CO

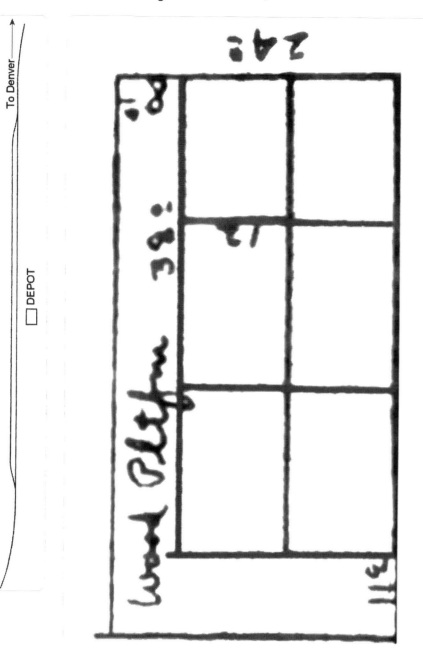

To Denver

☐ DEPOT

24'

38'

8'

Wood Platform

12'

ELEVATION 10028'

DEPOT

Built: Not Available
Construction: One-story frame structure of 24' x 38'.
Roof: Gable, wood shingles.
Walls: Board and batten.

Destroyed by fire October 11 1926.

DEPOT

97

ELEVATION 9510'

DEPOT

Built: Not Available.
Construction: One-story frame structure of 24' x 36'.

Retired by 1900.

Garfield, CO

Monarch, CO

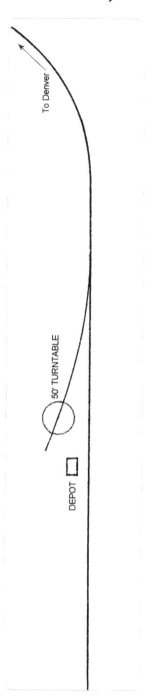

DEPOT

Built: 1884.
Construction: One-story frame structure of 16' x 24'.
Roof: Gable, wood shingles.
Walls: Board and batten.

Abandoned prior to 1920.
Retired and sold 1922.

FREIGHT HOUSE

Built: Not Available.
Construction: Frame structure of 16' x 20'.
Converted to bunk house.

Retired 1939.

Marshall Pass, CO

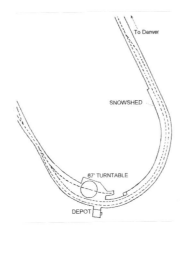

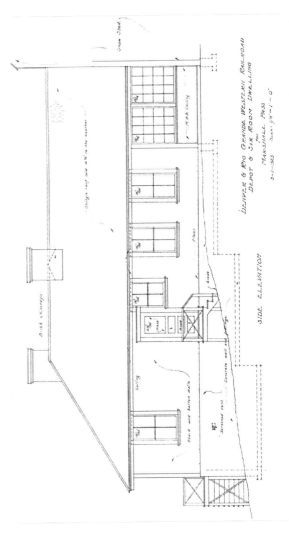

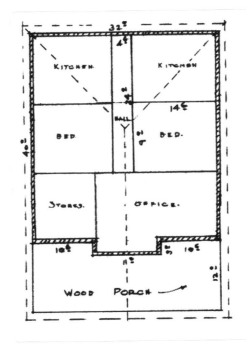

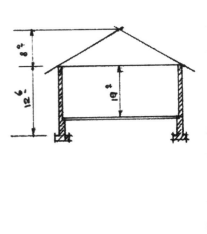

Sargent, CO

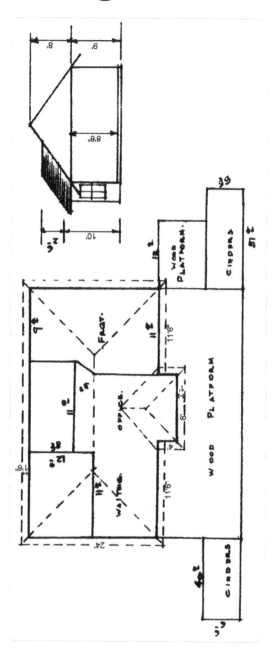

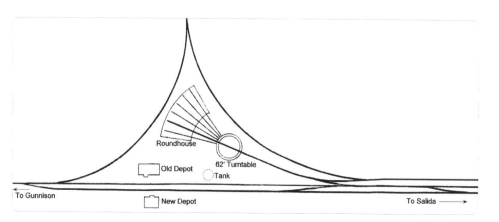

FIRST DEPOT

Built: Not Available.
Construction: One-story frame 20' x 60'.

Destroyed by fire 1904.

SECOND DEPOT

Built: Originally built 1889.
Moved from Chester 1904.
Construction: One-story frame 24' x 31', with an addition of 4' x 8'. Freight room extended 24' x 14' in 1920.
Roof: Hip, wood shingles.
Walls: Board and batten.

Retired 1953.

EATING HOUSE

Built: By 1891.
Construction: Frame of 20' x 45'. Additions of 12' x 21', 8' x 15' and 8' x 18'.

DEPOT

Moved: From Curcanti about 1901.
Construction: One-story frame of 24' x 27', with 10' x 14' and 5' x 11' additions.
Roof: Hip, wood shingles.
Walls: Lap siding.

Retired and sold 1946.

Doyle, CO

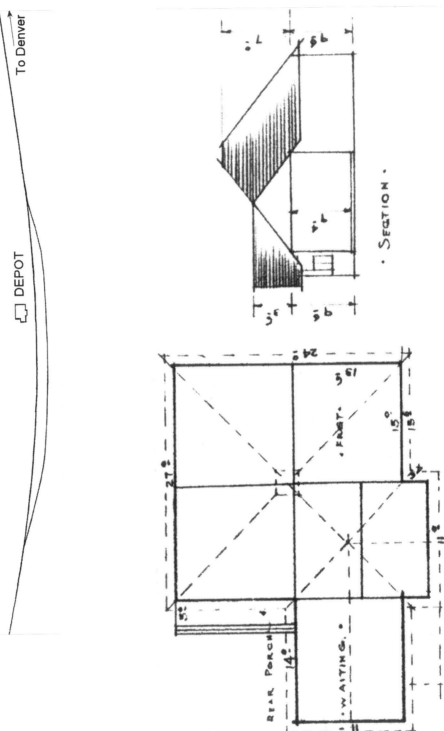

Parlin, CO

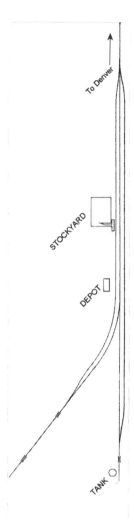

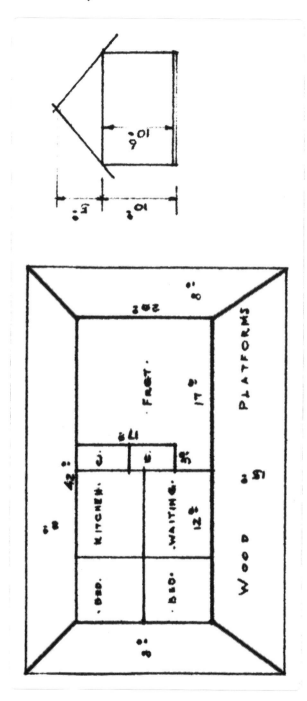

ELEVATION 7952'

DEPOT

Built: 1888.
Construction: One-story frame structure of 20' x 42'.
Roof: Gable, wood shingles.
Walls: Board and batten.

Retired 1953.

Gunnison, CO

ELEVATION 7683'

PASSENGER DEPOT

Built: 1883.
Construction: Frame
24' x 154' (not D&RGW
property). Passenger
depot located in La
Veta Hotel, Gunnison.

SEPERATE EXPRESS
AND BAGGAGE
BUILDING

Construction: 16' x 32'.
Roof: Wood shingles.
Wall: Board and
batten.

FREIGHT DEPOT

Built: 1883.
Construction: Frame
structure of 24' x 200'.
Roof: Wood shingles.
Walls: Board & batten.

Both passenger and
freight depots were
retired in 1931.
Replaced by a new
passenger and freight,
brick and concrete,
depot of 25' x 141' as
shown in plans.

104

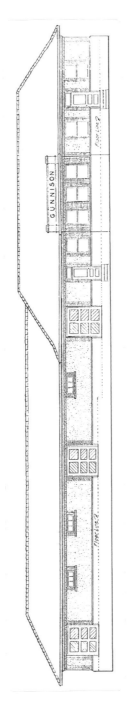

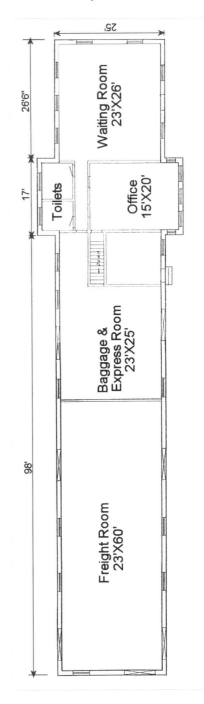

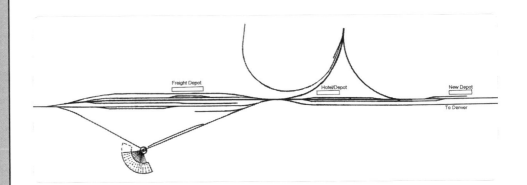

Parlin ↗

Gunnison ↗

Sargent ↗

Gunnison ↗

KEZAR TO WHITEWATER

Miles from Denver
to:

Kezar................. 300.08	Olathe.......... 362.21
Sapinero............. 313.97	Delta........... 372.83
Cimarron........... 329.01	Roubideau... 377.53
Cerro Summit..... 334.59	Dominguez.. 390.92
Cedar Creek........ 341.27	Whitewater.. 411.80
Montrose........... 351.51	

Kezar, CO

ELEVATION 7434'

DEPOT

Built: Not Available.
Construction: One-story frame structure of 11' x 14'. Additions of 11' x 20' and 12' x 35'.

Retired by 1900.

Sapinero, CO

DEPOT

Built: 1889.
Construction: One-story frame structure of 22' x 76' with 4' x 10' addition.
Used for both depot and dwelling.
Roof: Gable, wood shingles.
Walls: Board and batten.

Retired 1953.

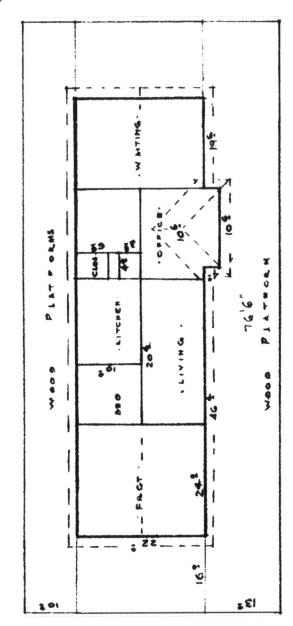

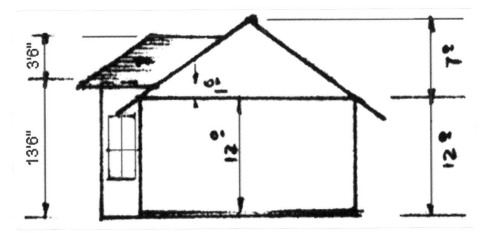

Cimmaron, CO

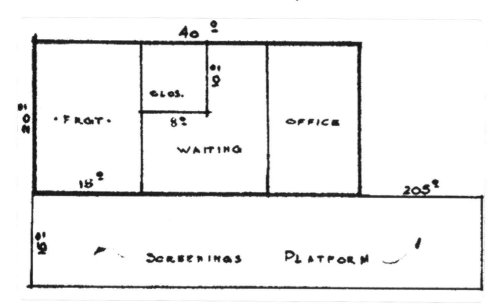

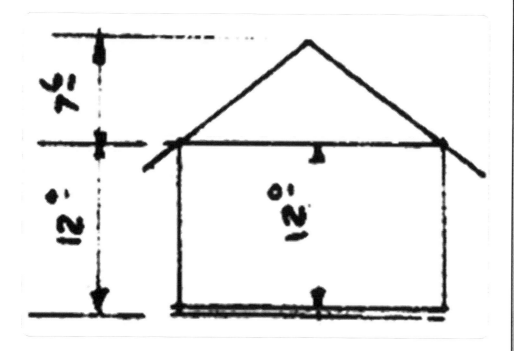

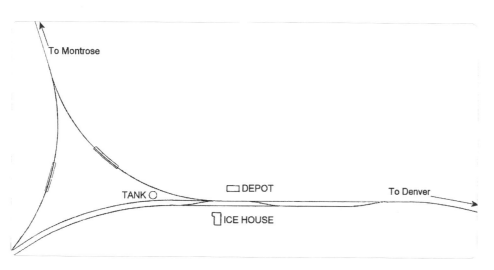

ELEVATION 6906'

DEPOT

Built: Not Available.
Construction: One-story frame structure of 20'X40'.
Roof: Gable, wood shingles.
Walls: Lap siding with 2'6" M&B wainscot.

Retired 1949.

Cerro Summit, CO

DEPOT

Built: 1890.
Construction: One-story frame structure of 12' x 41', with 6' x 9' bay window and 9' x 12' lean-to.
Roof: Gable, wood shingles.
Walls: Board and batten.

Retired 1938.

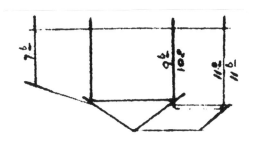

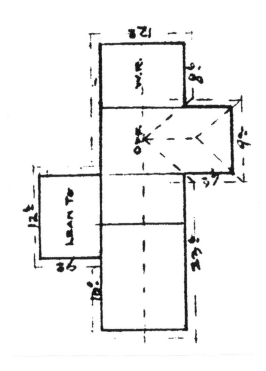

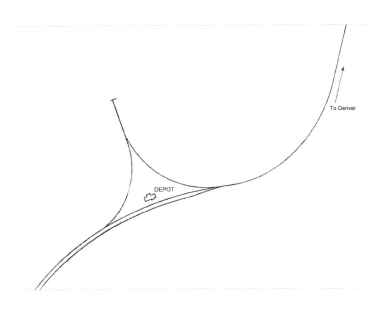

DEPOT

To Denver

110

Cedar Creek, CO

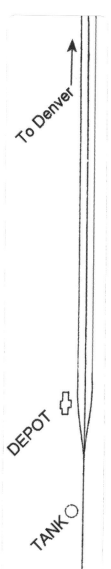

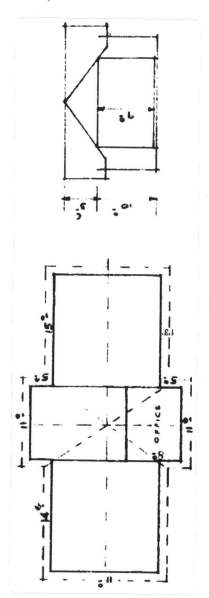

TELEGRAPH OFFICE

Built: Not Available.
Construction: One-story frame structure of 11' x 40'.
Roof: Gable, wood shingles.
Walls: Lap siding.

Used as a bunkhouse by 1920.

Retired 1938.

Montrose, CO 1-2

ELEVATION 5811'

FIRST PASSENGER DEPOT

Built: 1886.
Construction: One-story frame of 23' x 62'.
Roof: Gable, wood shingles.
Walls: Board and batten.
Canopy: Wood shingles.

Remodelled as freight depot c1912 to replace original freight depot.

SECOND PASSENGER DEPOT

Built: 1912.
Construction: Passenger and baggage structure of 25' x 105', with a 9' x 38' addition.
Walls: Cement/plaster.
Roof: Hip, red tiles.
Walls: Stucco finish.

Retired 1973.

THIRD PASSENGER DEPOT

A 12'X32' prefabricated building was installed in 1973.

112

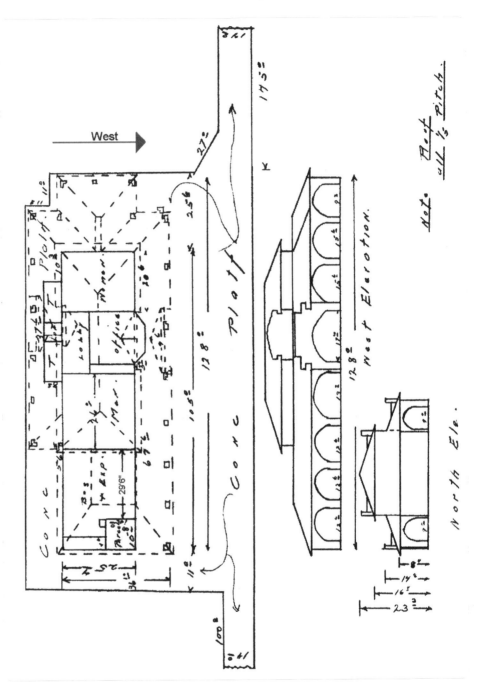

West

Montrose, CO 2-2

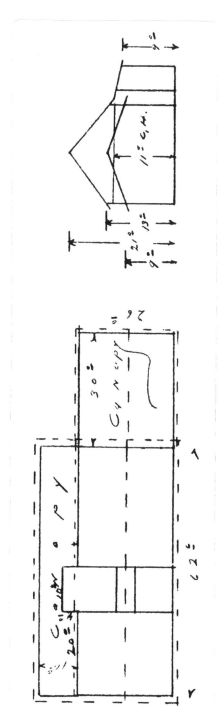

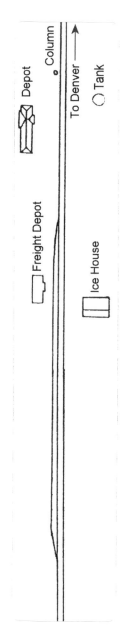

FIRST FREIGHT
DEPOT

Built: c1886.
Construction: One-
story frame structure
frame of 20'X40'.
Burned April 18 1910.

SECOND FREIGHT
DEPOT

First passenger depot
remodelled as freight
depot c1912.

Retired 1959.

113

Olathe, CO

FIRST DEPOT

Built: 1895.
Construction: One-story frame structure of 20' x 48'.
Roof: Gable, wood shingles.
Walls: Board and batten.
Rearranged and extended 1924.

Retired 1947.

SECOND DEPOT

Built: 1947.
Construction: Modern depot type with a flat roof.
Walls: Asbestos-cement shingle walls on siding.
Roof: Tar-gravel.

Retired 1972.

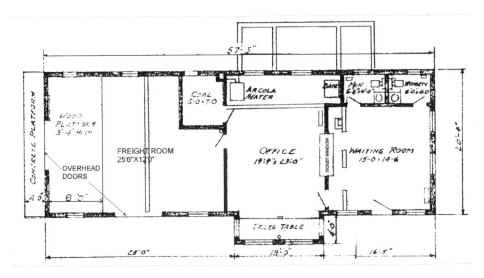

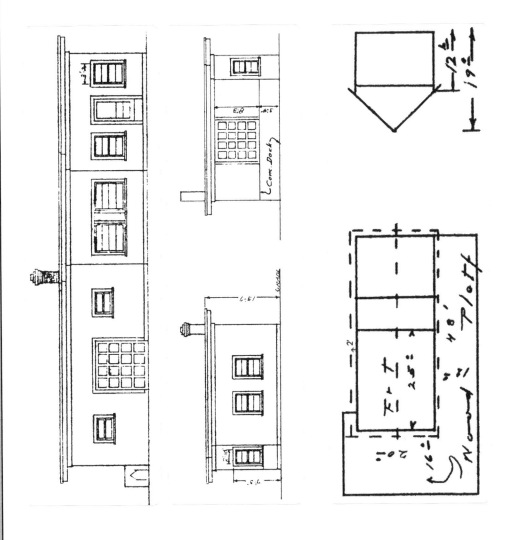

Delta, CO

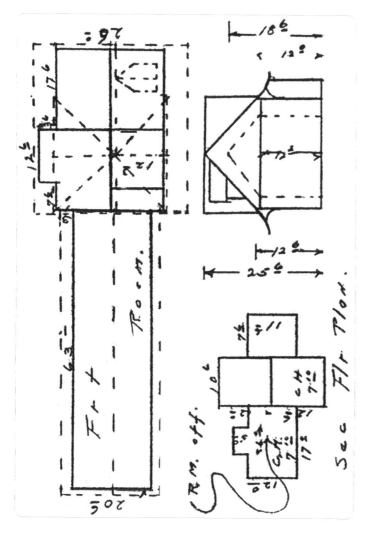

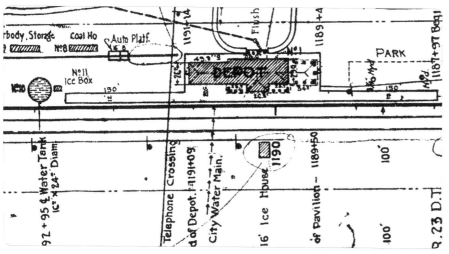

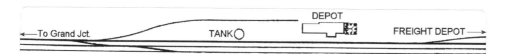

FIRST DEPOT

Built: Not Available.

Construction: Two-story frame structure of 26' x 37'. With one-story 20' x 63' & 3'6" x 12' additions.
Roof: Wood shingles.
Walls: Drop siding.

Moved 1918 and remodeled as a freight depot.

SECOND DEPOT

Built: 1918.
Construction: One-story brick structure of 29' x 125', with 34' pavilion.
(Note: Dimensions are approximate.)
Roof: Hip, tiles.
Walls: Brick.

Retired 1967.

THIRD DEPOT

Built 1967.
Construction: Metal structure of 16' x 20'.
Walls: Metal.

FREIGHT DEPOT

Converted from first depot 1918.

Retired 1958.

Dominguez, CO

ELEVATION 4801'

TELEGRAPH STATION

Built: By 1891.
Construction: One-story frame structure of 12' x 20'.

Retired by 1900.

Rubideau, CO

ELEVATION 4904

DEPOT

Built: By 1891.
Construction: One-story frame structure of 12' x 21'.

Retired by 1900.

Whitewater, CO

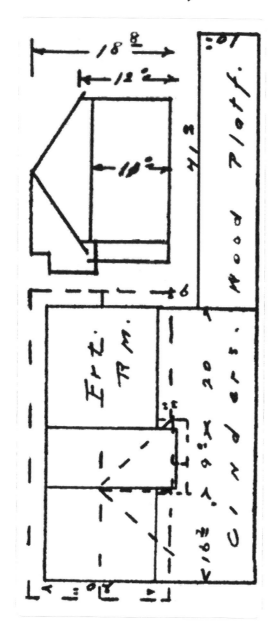

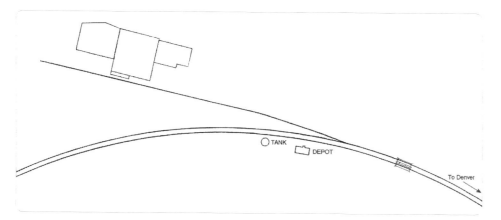

Photos 13

Cimmaron ↗

Montrose (rear) ↗

Sapinero ↗

Montrose (front) ↗

VILLA GROVE TO ALAMOSA

Miles from Denver
to:

Villa Grove...................... 245.43

Mineral Hot Springs........ 250.93

Moffat............................. 262.26

Hooper............................ 280.27

Mosca.............................. 286.84

Alamosa........................... 300.84

Villa Grove, CO

FIRST DEPOT

Built by 1891.
Construction: One-story frame structure of 20' x 72'.

SECOND DEPOT

Built (or rebuilt) 1901.
Construction: One-story frame of 24' x 70'.
Roof: Hip, composition No.2.
Walls: Board and batten.

Retired 1940.

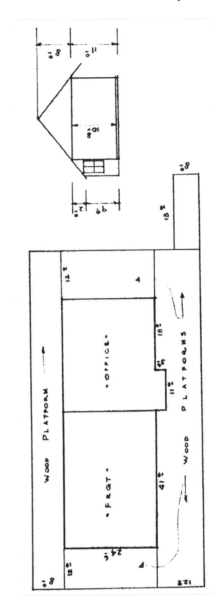

Depot   To Denver →

Mineral Hot Springs, CO

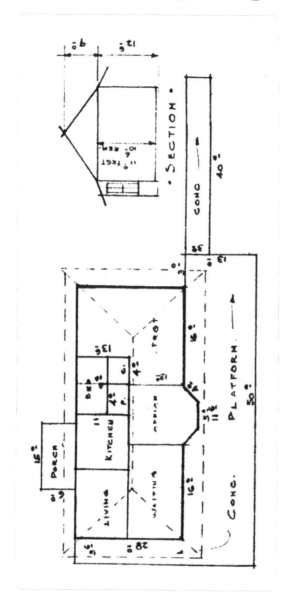

ELEVATION 7767'

DEPOT

Built: 1916.
Construction: One-story frame structure of 28' x 44'.
Roof: Hip, composition No.1.
Walls: Lap siding with 4'4" drop siding wainscot.

Retired 1940.

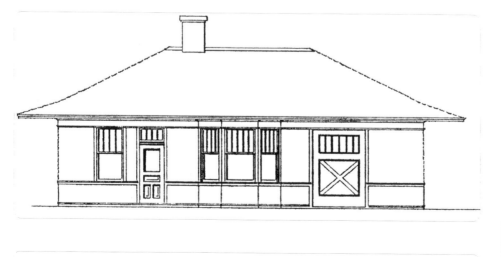

To Alamosa ⟶

☐ DEPOT

Moffat, CO

DEPOT

Built: 1890.
Construction: Two-story frame structure of 24' x 124', with additions of 4' x 24' and 4' x 11'.
Roof: Gable, wood shingles.
Walls: Lap siding with 3'6" M&B wainscot.

Destroyed by fire December 6 1940. Replaced September 1941 by a converted 18'X28' bunk house.

To Alamosa

Depot

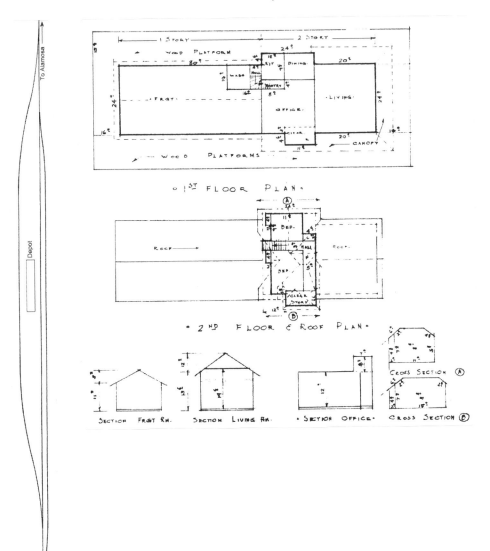

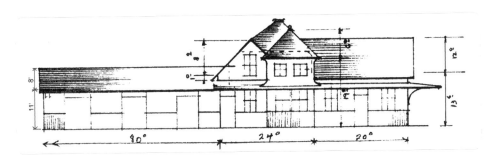

Hooper, CO

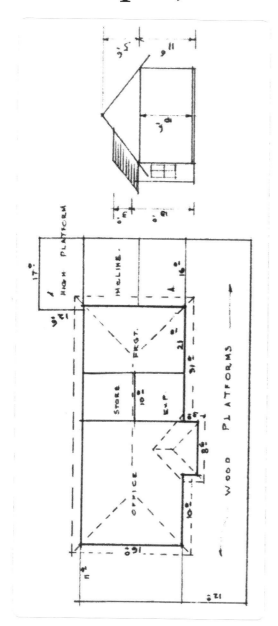

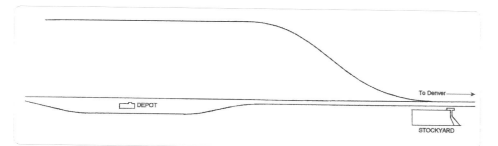

ELEVATION 7576'

DEPOT

Built: 1890.
Construction: One-story frame structure of 16' x 49', with a 3'X9' addition.
Roof: Hip, wood shingles.
Walls: Board and batten.

Retired 1955.

Mosca, CO

DEPOT

Built: 1890.
Construction: One-story frame structure of 24' x 36', with a 10' x 14' addition.
Roof : Gable, wood shingles.
Walls: Board and batten.

Retired 1941.

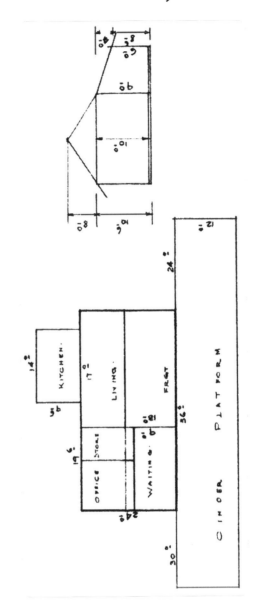

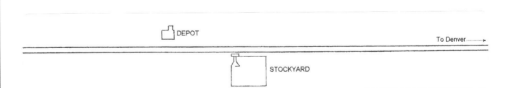

DEPOT

To Denver

STOCKYARD

Alamosa, CO

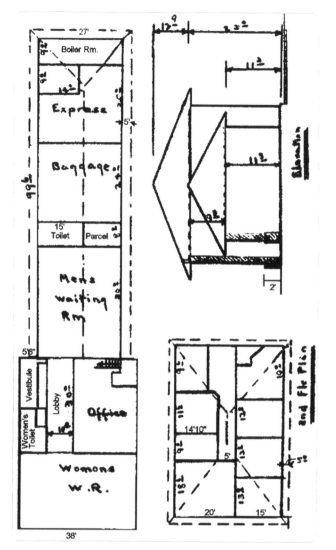

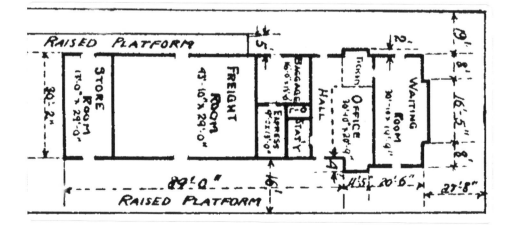

ELEVATION 7546'

DEPOT

Built: 1888.
Construction: One-story frame structure of 32' x 89', with a 22' x 25' office and waiting room.
1891 list shows 32'6" x 123' with waiting room 20' x 31'. With a Raised Platform on both sides.
Roof: Gable, wood shingles; waiting room metal.
Walls: Lap siding.

Destroyed by fire December 25 1907.

PASSENGER DEPOT

Built: 1909.
Construction: Two-story structure of 38' x 52' and one story of 27' x 99" structure.
Roof: Hip, tile.
Walls: Brick.

Retired 1961 and sold to city.

FREIGHT DEPOT

Built 1909.
Construction: Frame 25' x 90'.
Extended 1917 to 25' x 112'.
Roof: Composition.
Walls: Drop siding.

Passenger facilities added 1961.

Photos 14

Moffat

Alamosa (1893)

LA VETA TO BLANCA
(FOURTH DIVISION)

Miles from Denver
to:

    La Veta.............. 185.54

    La Veta Pass....... 202.39

    Fort Garland...... 222.92

    Blanca............... 227.63

La Veta, CO

ELEVATION 9242'

DEPOT

Moved from Placer (Russell) following redundancy in 1902. Construction: One-story frame 24' x 47'.

Destroyed by fire 1981.

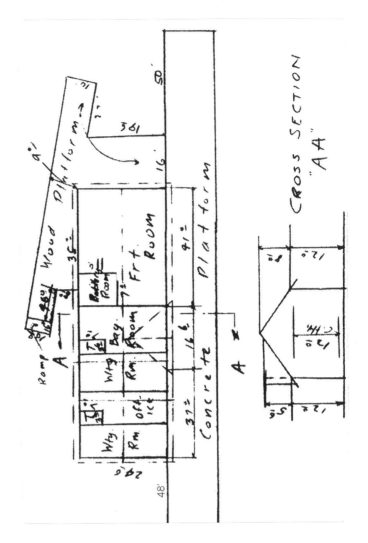

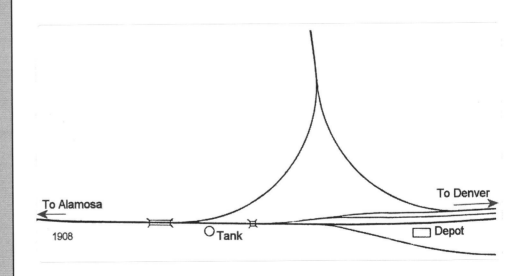

La Veta Pass, CO

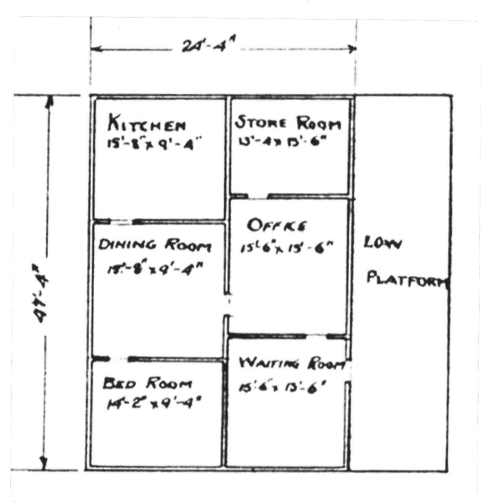

KITCHEN
15'-8" x 9'-4"

STORE ROOM
13'-4" x 13'-6"

DINING ROOM
15'-8" x 9'-4"

OFFICE
15'-6" x 13'-6"

LOW PLATFORM

BED ROOM
14'-2" x 9'-4"

WAITING ROOM
15'-6" x 13'-6"

24'-4"

47'-4"

DEPOT   To Denver →

ELEVATION:
Unknown

DEPOT

Built: By 1891.
Construction: One-story stone 15' x 27' with additions of 14' x 15' stone and 12' x 14' frame.

Fort Garland, CO

ELEVATION 7936'

FIRST DEPOT

Built: c1878.
Construction: One-story frame structure of 17' x 27', with a 12' x 27' addition.
Replaced 1888.

SECOND DEPOT

Built: 1888.
Construction: One-story frame structure of 16' x 72'.

Destroyed by fire December 29 1917. Narrow gauge combination smoker and baggage car 8' x 25' temporarily substituted as a passenger depot and a 32' box car body for the freight depot.

THIRD DEPOT

Built: 1921.
Construction: One story frame structure of 20' x 90' With living room for agent.
No details available.

Retired 1968.

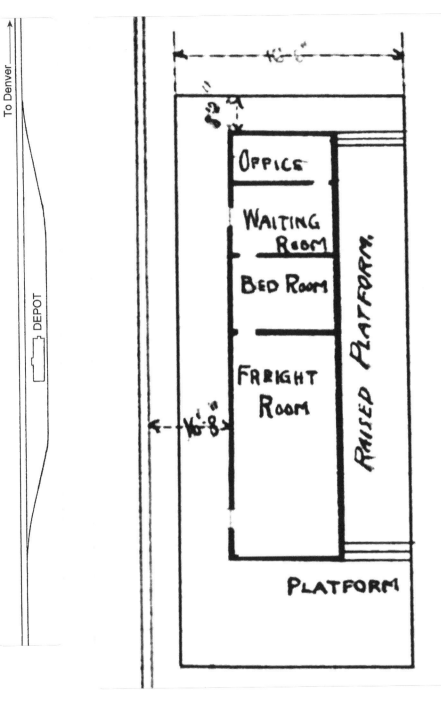

To Denver

DEPOT

OFFICE

WAITING ROOM

BED ROOM

FREIGHT ROOM

RAISED PLATFORM

PLATFORM

130

Blanca, CO

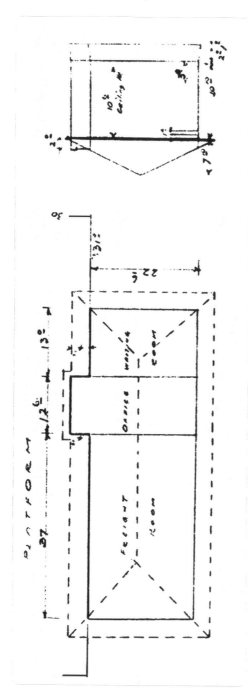

FIRST DEPOT

Built: Now Available.
Construction: Frame
structure of 20' x 30'.
Converted to
warehouse c1910.

Destroyed by fire July
4 1916.

SECOND DEPOT

Built 1910.
Construction: One-
story frame 22' x 62'.
Roof: Hip, wood
shingles.
Walls: Stucco finish
with 3'drop siding
wainscot.

Freight room retired
1961.
Remainder retired
1985.

Photos 15

La Veta Pass ↗
Blanca ↗

La Veta ↗
Fort Garland ↗

Branch Lines

Miles from Denver
to:

WESTCLIFFE
Westcliffe...............209.38

GRANEROS
Graneros...............163.14

ROUSE
Pryor....................182.88
Rouse....................184.02

BLUE RIVER
Kokomo.................294.25

ASPEN BRANCH
Carbondale............372.98
Aspen...................401.31

CRESTED BUTTE
Almont.................299.49
Crested Butte.........316.29

LAKE CITY
Lake City......................350.53

OURAY
Colona.........................363.84
Dallas..........................374.36
Ridgway........................377.08

NORTH FORK
Austin..........................380.86
Hotchkiss.....................397.74
Paonia.........................405.92
Somerset.......................415.28

CRESTONE
Crestone......................273.70

Westcliffe, CO

FIRST DEPOT

Built: 1886.
Construction: One-story approx of 20' x 67'.

SECOND DEPOT

Built 1901.
Construction: One and two story frame structure of 24' x 69', with a 4' x 11' bay window addition.
Roof: Hip, wood shingles.
Walls: Lap siding first story and wood shingles second story.

Retired 1938.

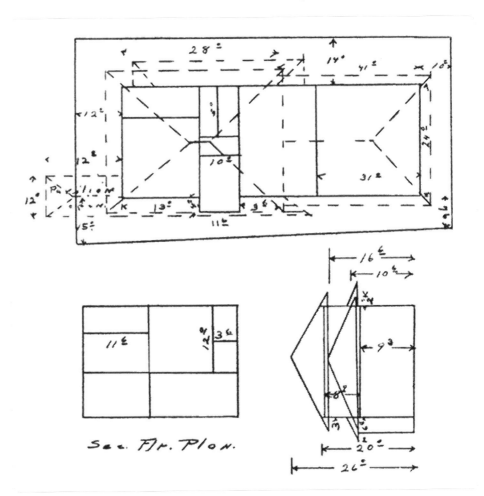

Sec. Flr. Plon.

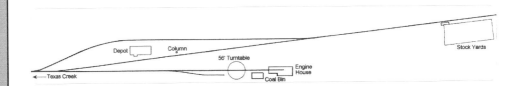

Graneros, CO

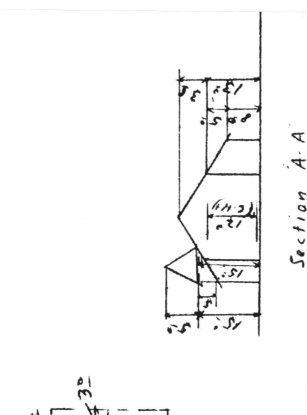

Section A-A

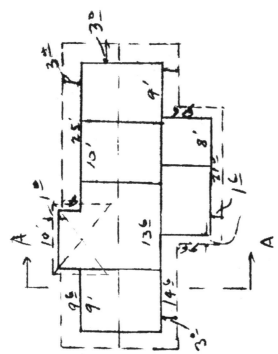

DEPOT

To Denver →

DEPOT

Built 1891.
Construction: One-story frame structure of 16' x 44'. With 10' x 12', 4' x 10' and 10' x 17' (porch) additions.
Roof: Gable, wood shingles.
Tower: Wood shingles.
Walls: Lap siding with 3' beaded wainscot.

Retired 1922.

ELEVATION
Unlisted

DEPOT

Built: Unlisted.
Construction: One-story frame structure 24' x 26' with a 4' x 24' porch.

Probably retired prior to 1920.

Pryor, CO

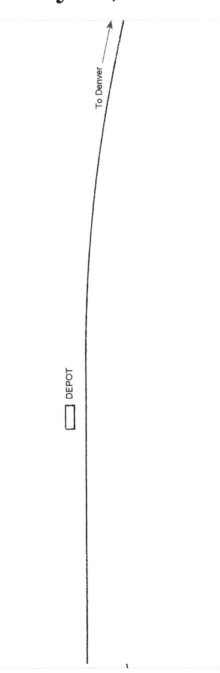

Rouse, CO

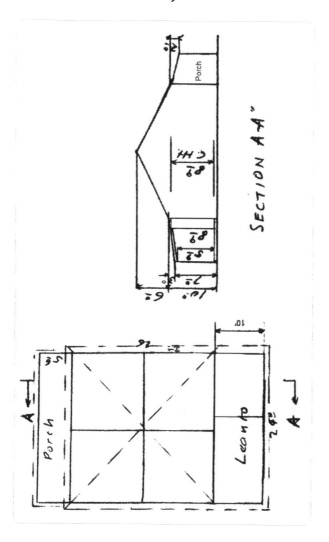

SECTION A-A"

ELEVATION 6473'

DEPOT

Built: Not Available.
Construction: One-
story frame 24' x 26'
with lean to 24' x 10'.
Roof: Hip, wood
shingles.
Walls: Lap siding.

Used as a section house
by 1920.

Retired: Not Available.

Kokomo, CO

DEPOT

Built: Unlisted.
Construction: One-story frame depot and dwelling 24' x 62'.
No depot plan available.

Branch leased to C. & S. Ry.

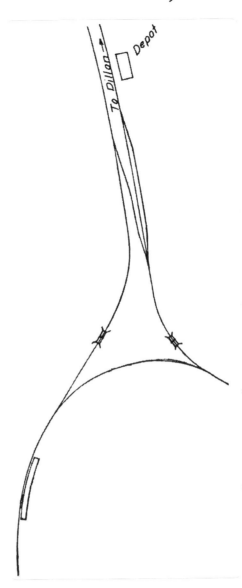

Carbondale, CO

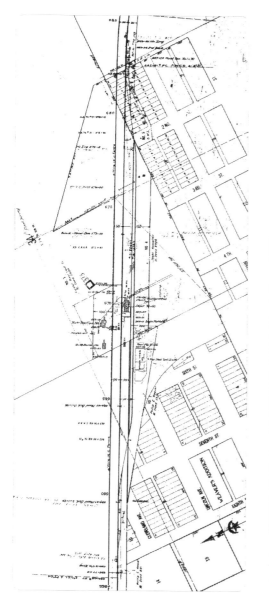

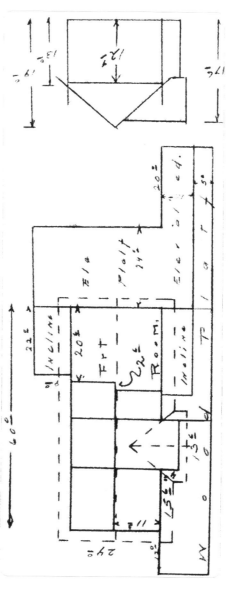

DEPOT

Built: 1888.
Construction: One-story frame structure of 24' x 60', with 4' x 13' addition.
Roof: Gable, wood shingles.
Walls: Lap siding.

Retired 1970.

ELEVATION 7874'

DEPOT

Built: 1888.
Construction: One-story frame structure of 16' x 76'.

Blown down by wind May 13 1913. Replaced by Colorado Midland Ry. Depot.

Aspen, CO

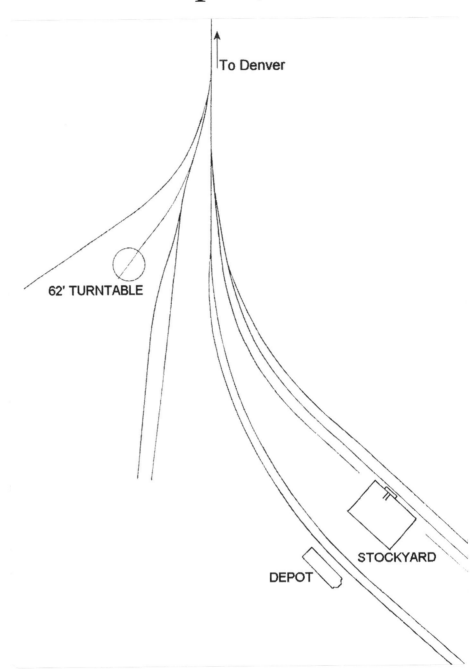

To Denver

62' TURNTABLE

STOCKYARD

DEPOT

Almont, CO

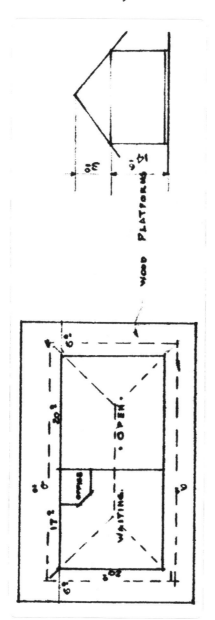

ELEVATION 8042'

DEPOT

Built: 1906.
Construction: One-story rustic frame structure of 20' x 37'.
Roof: Hip, corrugated iron.
Walls: Log slabs.

Retired 1945.

DEPOT

To Denver

Crested Butte, CO

DEPOT

Built: 1883.
Construction: Two-story frame structure of 26' x 37', with One-story additions of 20' x 32' and 4' x 12'.
Roof: Gable, wood shingles.
Walls: Drop siding with 4' M&B wainscot and wood shingled gables.

Retired 1953.

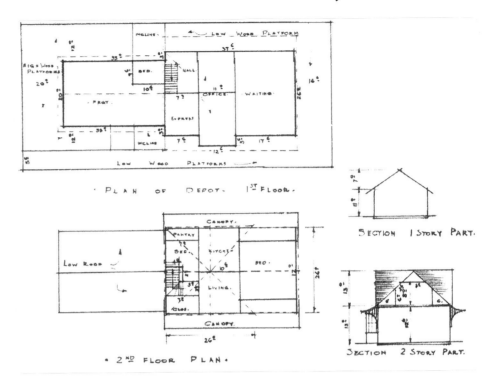

· PLAN OF DEPOT. 1ST FLOOR.·

· 2ND FLOOR PLAN·

SECTION 1 STORY PART.

SECTION 2 STORY PART.

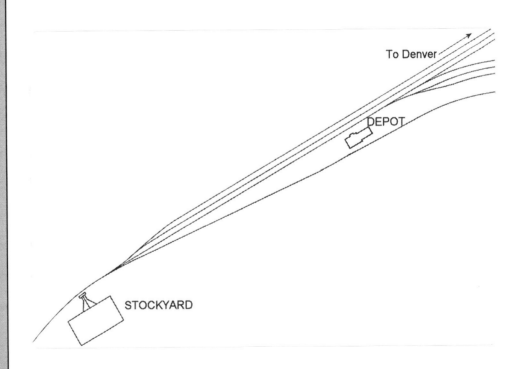

To Denver

DEPOT

STOCKYARD

Lake City, CO

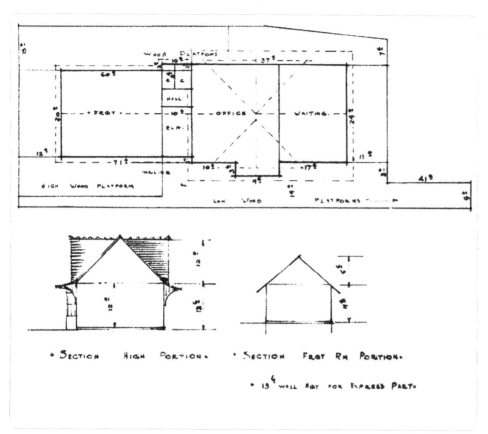

- SECTION HIGH PORTION·
- SECTION FRGT RM PORTION·
- 13 4 WALL RGT FOR EXPRESS PART·

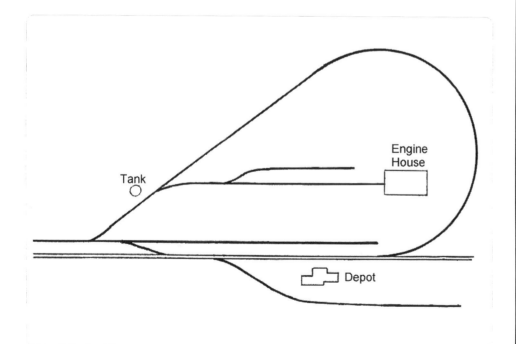

ELEVATION 8686'

DEPOT

Built: 1889.
Construction: One-story frame structure of 24' x 47', with additions of 20' x 60' and 3' x 9'.
Roof: Wood shingles.
Walls: Drop siding with 4' M&B wainscot; gables wood shingles.

Retired 1932.

ELEVATION 6409'

DEPOT

Built: Unlisted.
Construction: Frame
structure of 16' x 24'.
Roof: Wood shingles.

Retired 1939.

144

Colona, CO

DEPOT

To Denver →

STOCKYARD

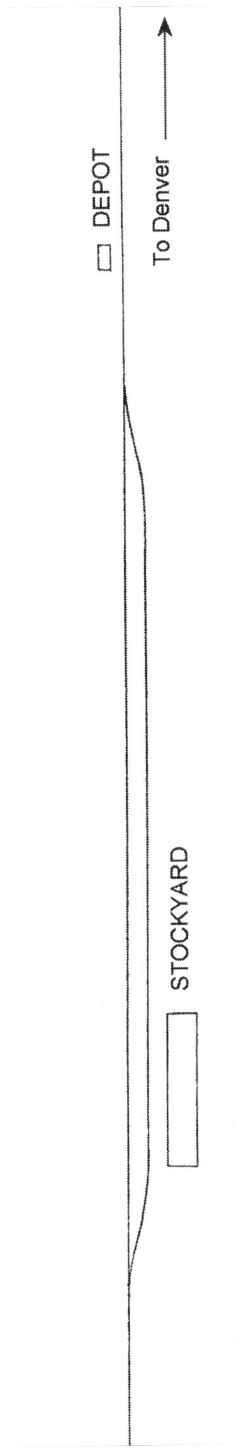

Dallas, CO

ELEVATION 6919'

DEPOT

Built: 1887.
Construction: One-story frame structure of 20' x 48'.

No agent by 1900.
(Depot absent from 1920 Valuation field notes.)

DEPOT

Built 1890.
Construction: Two story frame structure of 26' x 34'.
Additions of one-story 26' x 84' and two-story of 16' x 26' and 5' x 12'.
Roof: Gable, wood shingles.
Walls: Lap siding with 3'6" M & B wainscot and wood shingles in gables.

Retired 1965.

Ridgway, CO

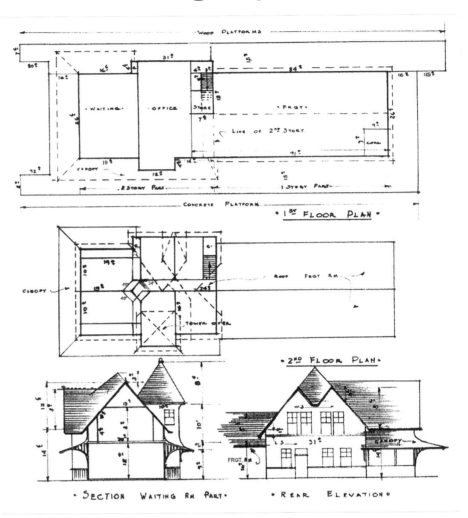

· 1ˢᵗ FLOOR PLAN ·

· 2ᴺᴰ FLOOR PLAN ·

· SECTION WAITING RM PART ·

· REAR ELEVATION ·

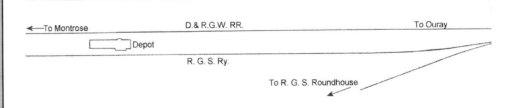

←To Montrose D.& R.G.W. RR. To Ouray

Depot

R. G. S. Ry.

To R. G. S. Roundhouse

Austin, CO

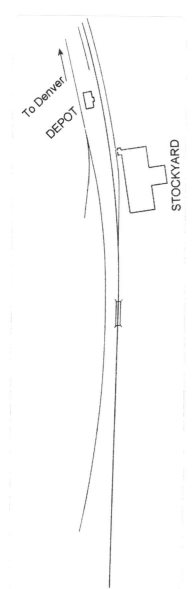

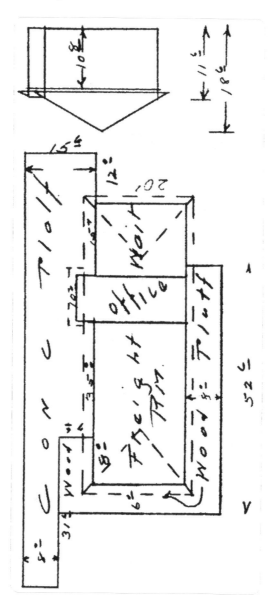

DEPOT

Built: 1909.
Construction: One-story frame structure of 20' x 40'.
Roof: Hip, wood shingles.
Walls: Lap siding.
Added freight room of 20'X20' in 1917.

Hotchkiss, CO

ELEVATION 5369'

DEPOT

Built: 1902.
Construction: One-story frame structure of 21' x 63', with 6' x 13' addition. (Similar to Paonia depot.)
Roof: Gable, wood shingles.
Walls: Lap siding.
A 21' x 23' addition made to freight room in 1913.

Remodeled 1953.
Retired 1970.

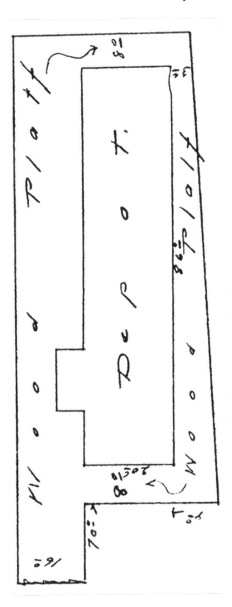

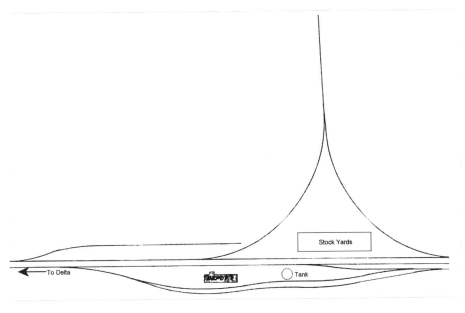

To Delta

Stock Yards

Tank

Paonia, CO

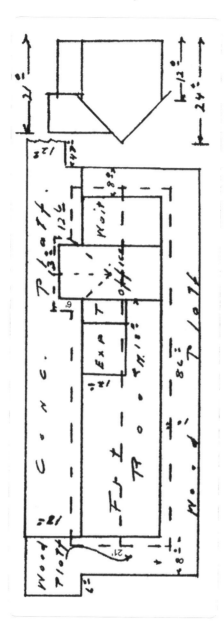

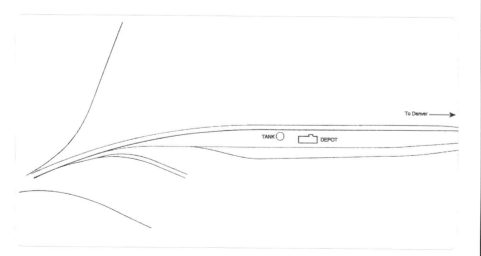

ELEVATION 5694'

DEPOT

Built: 1902.
Construction: One-story frame structure of 21' x 62', with a 6' x 13' addition. Addition of 21' x 24' to freight room 1913.
Roof: Gable, wood shingles.
Walls: Lap siding with 4' beaded wainscot.

Retired 1976.

ELEVATION 6065'

DEPOT

Built: 1903.
Construction: One-story frame structure of 18' x 48'.
Roof: Gable, wood shingles.
Walls Lap siding.

Retired 1969.

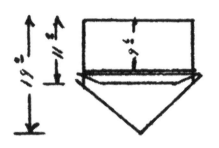

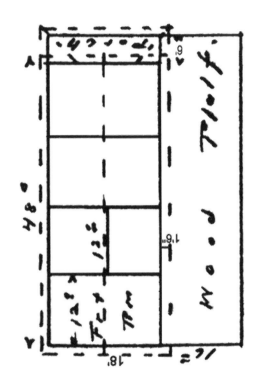

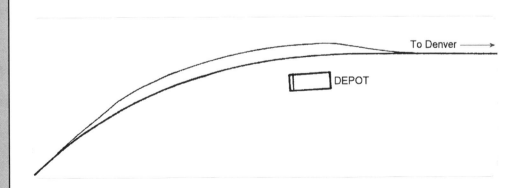

To Denver ⟶

DEPOT

Crestone, CO

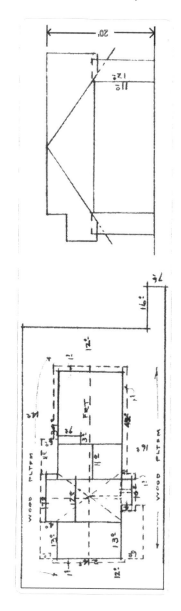

DEPOT

To Denver ⟶

ELEVATION 7881'

DEPOT

Built: 1901.
Construction: One-story frame structure of 24' x 69', with 4' x 17' and 4' x 10' bays.
Roof: Gable, wood shingles.
Walls: Board and batten.

Out of service 1913.
Retired and sold 1927.

Photos 16

Carbondale ↗
Crested Butte ↗

West Cliffe ↗
Aspen ↗

Photos 17

Hotchkliss ↗
Crestone ↘

Lake City ↗
Paonia ↘

ACKNOWLEDGMENTS

The authors are grateful to the Colorado Railroad Museum, Golden, CO, and the assistance provided by Kenton Forrest and Sharon McGee, for the information presented in this book.

INDEX

Numbers listed in parentheses are photos

INDEX

Numbers listed in parentheses are photos

Made in the USA
Columbia, SC
25 November 2017